"When I was just starting in ministry, no one shared his heart with me more than Lynn Anderson. He was a friend, a mentor, a guide, and an example. Now he has put into print what he has put into practice for forty years. Read and be blessed. The book is almost as good as the man."

— Rick Atchley, *senior minister, Richland Hills Church of Christ*

"I'm into my third decade of Lynn Anderson admiration. Few communicators speak with such tender conviction and practical admonition. This book, in particular, reminds us to steer away from stiff styles of corporate leadership and find our model in the tender-hearted pastor. Lynn has achieved this . . . by God's grace we can as well."

— Max Lucado, *senior minister, Oak Hills Church, and New York Times bestselling author*

"*They Smell Like Sheep* taught us *what* to do to be effective leaders and particularly effective shepherds. In *They Smell like Sheep, Volume 2,* Lynn Anderson provides wonderful insights and practical advice on *how* to cultivate our hearts in order to be effective leaders—Mesquite Bush Leaders."

— Ron Miller, *retired vice president, Procter & Gamble, and Hope Network board member*

What a difference a shepherd's heart can make! Thanks to Lynn Anderson for reminding us that effective leaders are service oriented, scripturally informed, sensitive to people, and strong in faith.

—David Faust, *President, Cincinnati Christian University*

"St. Paul tells young Timothy he is to be an example to his people—not a star or a celebrity. He is to be a living illustration of the gospel for young and old, and that is what Lynn Anderson has been for years for so many of us. He has lived out the heart of the gospel as a shepherd, mentor, preacher, author, and true example."

—Fred Smith, *President, The Gathering, www.thegathering.com*

Great missionaries immerse themselves into the life and culture of the people they go to serve. They are transformed into spiritual giants, blessed by God by giving themselves away. I know of no one who has immersed himself into the lives of leaders all over the nation more than Lynn Anderson. Through mentoring groups, retreats, and seminars, he has tirelessly served leaders when they hurt and when they heal. You can tell it when you read this book. The stories he shares, the issues he raises, and the practical reflective questions he gives the reader responds to the aspirations of every spiritual leader. This book is a great extension of Lynn's gift of giving hope and renewing a vision to be the best we can be in serving with the heart of our Great Shepherd.

—Evertt W. Huffard, *VP/Dean, Harding University Graduate School of Religion, Memphis*

Through the ages, God has called leaders who rarely possessed extraordinary competency, but always possessed extraordinary character.

In *They Smell Like Sheep, Volume 2,* Lynn masterfully unveils what this leader of extraordinary character looks like from the inside.

—Mark Kirk, *Partner, Linsalata Capital Partners and Hope Network Ministries Board Member*

Lynn Anderson calls us to "love well." Is that not what shepherd leadership is all about? In a post-Christendom culture where people are seeking Christ-like role models, may God supply us the grace 'to love well.' As Lynn encourages us, it's time to put religion aside and live out the gospel.

—Nancy Keeth, *Executive Minister, Fourth Avenue Church, Franklin, Tennessee*

"Few in Christendom understand the heart of a shepherd as does Lynn Anderson. Not only does he have a gift for articulating the concepts of servant leadership, but he speaks from the experience of one who has accepted a call to shepherd the Shepherds of the church. *They Smell like Sheep, Volume 2,* along with *They Smell like Sheep,* should be in the library of anyone who has accepted the responsibility and blessing of being a Christian leader."

—Jackie L. Halstead, PhD, *Chair, Department of Marriage and Family Therapy, Abilene Christian University*

In his second volume on shepherding God's people, Lynn Anderson draws us to holy places where we discover who we are in God's presence and who we have been called to serve. In so doing he helps us tend to our own hearts as we tend to the lambs in our care and keeping.

D'Esta Love, *University Chaplain, Pepperdine University, Malibu, California*

Dr. Lynn Anderson

THEY SMELL LIKE SHEEP

VOLUME 2

Leading with the Heart of a Shepherd

HOWARD BOOKS
A DIVISION OF SIMON & SCHUSTER
New York   London   Toronto   Sydney

Our purpose at Howard Books is to:
- *Increase faith* in the hearts of growing Christians
- *Inspire holiness* in the lives of believers
- *Instill hope* in the hearts of struggling people everywhere

Because He's coming again!

Published by Howard Books, a division of Simon & Schuster, Inc.
1230 Avenue of the Americas, New York, NY 10020
www.howardpublishing.com

They Smell Like Sheep, Volume 2 © 2007 by Lynn Anderson

13 Digit ISBN: 978-1-4516-3631-4

10 9 8 7 6 5 4 3 2 1

HOWARD colophon is a registered trademark of Simon & Schuster, Inc.

Manufactured in the United States of America

For information regarding special discounts for bulk purchases, please contact: Simon & Schuster Special Sales at 1-800-456-6798 or business@simonandschuster.com.

Edited by Steve Halliday
Cover design by John Lucas
Interior design by John Mark Luke Designs

Scripture quotations not otherwise marked are from the *Holy Bible, New International Version* ®. Copyright © 1973, 1978, 1984 by International Bible Society. Used by permission of Zondervan. All rights reserved. Scripture quotations marked KJV are taken from the *Holy Bible, King James Version*. Scripture quotations marked MSG are taken from *The Message*. Copyright © 1993, 1994, 1995, 1996, 2000, 2001, 2002. Used by permission of NavPress Publishing Group. Scripture quotations marked NLT are taken from the *Holy Bible, New Living Translation*, copyright © 1996. Used by permission of Tyndale House Publishers, Inc., Wheaton, Illinois 60189. All rights reserved. Scripture quotations marked NASB are from the *New American Standard Bible*®. Copyright © 1960, 1962, 1963, 1968, 1971, 1972, 1973, 1975, 1977, 1995 by The Lockman Foundation. Used by permission. Scripture quotations marked NKJV are from the *New King James Version*®. Copyright © 1982 by Thomas Nelson, Inc. Used by permission. All rights reserved. Italics in scriptures were used by the author for emphasis.

A spiritual leader is the kind of person
God-hungry people want to be like.

—Lynn Anderson

To Hope Network friends,
without whose encouragement this book
would likely never have happened.

Krista Bates	David Culp	Ron Miller
Randy Boggs	Phil Eubanks	Dean Owen
Billy Busch	Blair Francis	John Samuel
Byron Carlock	Jon Halbert	Gary Skidmore
Brad Cheves	David House	Jimmy Smith
Brent Clifton	Barbara Hunter	Carole Tolbert
Reggie Crawford	Royce Hunter	Diane Treusdell
	Mark Kirk	

Woe to the shepherds of Israel who only take care of themselves! Should not shepherds take care of the flock? You eat the curds, clothe yourselves with the wool and slaughter the choice animals, but you do not take care of the flock. You have not strengthened the weak or healed the sick or bound up the injured. You have not brought back the strays or searched for the lost. You have ruled them harshly and brutally. So they were scattered because there was no shepherd, and when they were scattered they became food for all the wild animals. My sheep wandered over all the mountains and on every high hill. They were scattered over the whole earth, and no one searched or looked for them.

Therefore . . . as surely as I live, declares the Sovereign LORD, because my flock lacks a shepherd and so has been plundered and has become food for all the wild animals, and because my shepherds did not search for my flock but cared for themselves rather than for my flock . . . I will rescue my flock from their mouths, and it will no longer be food for them.

—Ezekiel 34:2–10

CONTENTS

CONTENTS

C. GENE WILKES

I met Lynn outside a conference room near Colorado Springs one spring. We had both arrived late to a meeting of church leaders for peer interaction and encouragement. As we introduced ourselves and told our stories, I soon realized God had graced my life by my delayed entrance to the meeting. I had met someone with whom my heart beat, and I had been introduced to a leader whom I wanted as a mentor in my life. Years, geography, and experiences had separated our lives up until that meeting, but we soon discovered that God had us both on the same path: a desire to know and live out a biblical model of leadership for those who were called to lead in Christ's church.

A few years after that meeting, I followed Lynn around the U.S. to some of his peer learning groups. He had written *They Smell Like Sheep* by that time, and our friendship had deepened. Like Barnabas, whose name means "Son of Encouragement" and who invited Saul of Tarsus to join him in ministry at Antioch, Lynn invited me to join him as he served leaders whom he mentored and cared for in monthly gatherings. As I sat with him in the day-long groups, I observed a proven leader who genuinely cared for those he led, and *I saw a shepherd who loved his sheep*. Lynn embodied what he had called each of us to embrace. His words were not idle musings about an era gone by where shepherds who cared for smelly sheep was the primary metaphor for leadership among God's people. He lived what he taught and called others to emulate him.

Leadership for those in the church has become an industry unto itself. Thousands summit yearly to hear leaders of business, ministries, and churches tell how to apply marketplace, church growth, and personal practices to ministry in order to experience "success" in the hearer's place of service. Book titles with adjectives like "missional," "next level," "visionary," and even "spiritual" describe leadership for those who lead in the church. We have laws and principles of leadership gleaned from success stories of growing and transitioning ministries. Journals and articles enumerate practical steps to lead people on mission and how to survive the struggles of leading people to reach goals and objectives. Personalities who lead large and growing ministries challenge our own makeup as leaders, and some of us wonder if we will ever measure up to all the lists leaders are to be and do.

Lynn passionately calls leaders in the church to return to the biblical model of leader as shepherd. This invitation has captured the hearts of those who long for something more than the latest model and practices of leadership. The enduring acceptance of *They Smell Like Sheep* springs from its uncompromising (yet nonjudgmental) call to return to the biblical example of leader as shepherd. Yes, we have been told the metaphor is from an age gone by and that we have learned so much more since those ancient days of patiently tending animals by one committed to their care, but the timeless truth of Jesus's example and teachings still apply to those who call him Leader and Mentor today. Jesus called himself the Shepherd (John 10:11), and apprentices of Jesus like Peter instructed their followers to lead as the "Head Shepherd" had led (1 Peter 5:1–4). The "ancient-future ring" of this call to lead like Jesus challenges our modern and postmodern methods of leadership, but Lynn will not allow us to cast off Jesus's model of leadership as we would a yellow, coffee-stained newspaper that we had kept because it held a story of an admired leader we once longed to be like.

In this *Volume 2* of *They Smell Like Sheep*, Lynn addresses the starting and ending place of leadership among God's people: the heart of a leader. He leads us once again to Jesus as our model of leadership, and he refuses to veer from that example. He leads us through the pages of Scripture that convict and encourage those of us who desire to lead like the Shepherd, and he gives us exercises to strengthen our hearts as we do the difficult yet rewarding work of shepherding the people of God. Follow Lynn's lead and you will discover how to lead those in your care.

They Smell Like Sheep, Volume 2, is the next lesson on a leader's journey to become like Jesus. Please enter its pages with the hope that you have someone who has the heart of a shepherd and who sees himself first as a sheep loved and led by the Shepherd.

C. Gene Wilkes, PhD
Senior Pastor, Legacy Church, Plano, Texas
Author, *Jesus on Leadership* and *Paul on Leadership*
September 15, 2006

foreword

BOB RUSSELL

When I was in fourth grade our church got a new preacher who significantly impacted my life. He was just twenty-four years old and quite a contrast to the eighty-three-year-old minister who had just retired. I loved Brother Bob Phillips. I'm sure some older believers thought his preaching was shallow since he was so young and just beginning, but when he preached, he told stories that I understood and could apply to my life. He used humor and laughed and was so human that he made the Christian life appealing. *If I ever become a preacher, that's the way I would preach*, I found myself thinking even as a ten-year-old.

But what impressed me most about Bob Phillips was that he was a shepherd who had a heart for his sheep. My favorite memory of him is of one evening when I was in the dugout, getting ready for a Little League baseball game. I was really surprised to see Brother Bob standing outside the right-field fence all by himself. No one else on our team belonged to his church. He just came to see me play! I couldn't get over that.

One Friday night after an active week at Deep Valley Christian service camp, Bob Phillips somehow sensed I was very troubled. An appeal had gone out for young men to make commitments to become preachers of the gospel. I hadn't "felt the call" and felt guilty about it. Bob sat down next to me and suggested that although I had not gone forward along with many others that it was okay. He would be praying that if God laid it on my heart to become a preacher in the future that I would be submissive to his will, because I would "make a good one."

I can't remember two paragraphs of what he preached, but his heart for God, his devotion to Christ, his personal integrity, and his love of people helped to shape my life and ministry for the next five decades.

In recent years Lynn Anderson has been that kind of shepherd to thousands of people. If anyone knows how to love the flock even though "they smell like sheep," it's Lynn. If anyone knows how to speak directly to the heart of the shepherd, it's Lynn.

This book goes deeper than just gimmicks and techniques of leadership. It's about the character and the heart of the leader. That's what perceptive people sense quickly and what even novices notice with the passing of time. It's the heart that makes the difference in an effective Sunday school teacher, youth coach, elder, small-group leader, parent, grandparent, Christian school teacher.

Spiritual sheep, stray sheep, and searching sheep aren't nearly so concerned about the knowledge and skill of the shepherd as they are his heart. When the sheep are in crisis, they go to a shepherd in whom they discern God's heart. This happens in weddings, funerals, family crises, at the hospital, and even when a little boy strikes out at a Little League baseball game with the bases loaded in the last inning. Jesus said the sheep would know their shepherd's voice and be drawn to it. It is the heart behind the voice that soothes and comforts God's people.

How do you measure the influence of one godly shepherd? I know this—it is the heart of the shepherd that most powerfully shapes lives and souls in our flocks. I commend Lynn's book to anyone who wishes to have his or her own heart shaped. Solomon wrote, "Above all else, guard your heart, for it is the wellspring of life" (Proverbs 4:23).

Bob Russell
Retiree Senior Minister, Southeast Christian Church, Louisville, Kentucky
Author of more than a dozen books, including *When God builds a Church*.

acknowledgments

Solomon said, "There is nothing new under the sun." This includes books. No book is entirely original—certainly not this one. Inspiration and ideas come from sources too numerous to mention. But special thanks to Rick Atchley, Carlus Gupton, H. B. London, Jon Mullican, Henri Nouwen, Eugene Peterson, Anne Silkman, Gary Southern, Brad Tuggle, Roger Weems, Gene Wilkes, and Dean Owen.

John Donne said, "No man is an island." This includes authors. A long list of people helped put this book together:

Allison Bagley, who spent months cheerfully tracking down sources, giving creative and editorial input, and writing letters.

Rick Brown, Norm Goodyear, Joe Hale, Scott Hanson, Royce Hunter, Don Jackson, Eddie Levick, Don Litton, Dean Owen, and Greg Taylor, who read the rough manuscript and gave invaluable input.

Plus, three hundred alumni of mentoring groups who prayed the project through, told stories, and cheered me on.

And thousands of men and women, moms and dads, small-group leaders and Sunday-school teachers—good shepherds, all—whose life stories shout encouragement. As with my book *They Smell Like Sheep*, the stories here tell of real people. Some are named with their permission. In some cases, however, I have combined one story with another or assigned fictitious names and shuffled genders and venues to protect anonymity, while retaining the point.

And, of course, Carolyn, co-originator of my best thoughts, who kept putting great ideas, pungent quotes—and fresh coffee—in front of me.

Above all, thank You, Great Shepherd of us all.

ASSUMPTIONS

We see at least two broad categories of leaders growing on the pages of the Bible: *Banyan Tree* leaders and *Mesquite Bush* leaders.

An old Indian proverb says, "Nothing grows under the banyan tree." Thick foliage on a banyan keeps sun and rain off any seedlings that fall near the tree. Consequently, banyans don't grow in thickets. Rather, you see one towering alone here, another standing way over there.

Not so, mesquite bushes! Their long taproots reach deep down to draw subterranean moisture. They have little foliage to block the sun and rain, so most seeds they drop germinate quickly. Plus, each bush throws off bushels of seeds. Even if a seed falls on a hot rock, a mesquite bush may spring up there by the end of the season. Consequently, like rabbits, they multiply swiftly and then multiply again and again.

God calls a few Banyan Tree leaders—strong, stand-alone persons who tend to tower over those around them. One of these led every major move of God in history. Think of Moses or Joshua, Paul or Peter, Augustine, John Calvin, Martin Luther, or John Wesley . . . Alexander Campbell, Martin Luther King Jr., Billy Graham, Chuck Swindoll, Bill Hybels, Rick Warren—just to name a few. These people led (or lead) movements or megachurches. But because they usually do not multiply themselves, they are few and far between.

No one need aspire to Banyan Tree leadership; God takes care of that. Banyans emerge only by his call and anointing, not by human career plans.

Anyone, however, can aspire to Mesquite Bush spiritual leadership.

introduction: ASSUMPTIONS

This is the kind God calls most. Mesquites do not necessarily stand out against the sky and rarely, if ever, lead movements or megachurches. But they are very good at producing and multiplying healthy, growing disciples of Jesus, who in turn keep multiplying.

This book is about Mesquite Bush leaders.

That means it is not just for "church leaders." Rather, this book aims for the hearts of all Christians who aspire to build people: moms and dads, Sunday school teachers, ministry leaders, small-group leaders, Bible study group leaders, Little League coaches, CEOs, and even quiet and private persons. Of course, it also includes church leaders such as elders, pastors, deacons, and ministers.

While this book is a sequel and its message can stand alone, to some degree *They Smell Like Sheep, Volume 2,* assumes that the reader has been exposed to the biblical, spiritual leadership principles spelled out in my earlier book, titled *They Smell Like Sheep.* That work emphasizes that spiritual leadership issues from character and is primarily about shepherding, mentoring, and equipping through relationships.

The wide interest stirred by *They Smell Like Sheep* frankly stunned me. Since its publication we have been overwhelmed with requests—from around the world and from various traditions—for seminars to train leaders in these biblical concepts.[1] Of course, this response reflects not so much on the quality of my book as it does the growing passion among Christian leaders to effectively prompt spiritual formation. Indeed, the biblical paradigm of spiritual leaders as shepherds, mentors, and equippers definitely appears to be "an idea whose time has *returned*!"

So this sequel goes beyond the original and aims to probe the hearts of effective shepherds and to offer some specific steps toward better shepherding.

This book leans heavily on stories. I interviewed more than two hundred key church leaders from across the United States and Canada, listening to stories from the lives of effective contemporary shepherds.

introduction: ASSUMPTIONS

Oh my, did the stories roll in! Thus, while these pages deal with some theory, I suspect that most readers will find the real-life "shepherd's heart" stories to be their favorite parts of the book. Even so, in the interest of space, some great stories ended up on the cutting-room floor. Apologies for that, in advance.

Naturally, this volume does not pretend to include everything important to the heart of a shepherd. I hope, however, that it will at least put some faces and feet on the theory of my prior book and will inspire rank-and-file Christ-followers to cultivate *the heart of a shepherd*.

Welcome to the journey.

A HEART
FOR GOD

Most high and glorious God, bring
light to the darkness of my heart . . .

—Francis of Assisi

one

THE HEART OF THE MATTER

Man looks at the outward appearance,
but the LORD looks at the heart.

—1 Samuel 16:7

My friend Brad writes,

Over thirty years ago a president engages his administration in a massive cover-up over a hotel break-in that eventually forces him to resign. Twenty-five years later another president wags his finger at the public and lies about an affair. Does character matter?

The CEO of a Fortune 500 company takes a small, upstart phone company, goes on a buying spree, and forms the second-largest communications company in history. He now faces up to eighty-five years in prison for cooking the company's books to the tune of $11 billion, wiping out thousands of investors in the process. Does character matter?

A brilliant physicist, who does research in molecular biology, leaves his prestigious office every day, goes home, and beats his wife senseless, because of his low self-esteem. Does character matter?

When Mother Teresa was asked about the utter futility of trying to feed millions of hungry people and rescuing the dying amid abject poverty in Calcutta, she responded, "God does not call us to be successful; he calls us to be faithful."

Yes, character matters. And it matters most of all in leadership, where Jesus talked a great deal about faithfulness versus success. When it comes to the heart of a shepherd, we can say with certainty, "Of course character does matter."[1]

So true! And character, dear reader, is a matter of the heart.

SPIRITUAL LEADERSHIP

April is a bright, young, multitasking, twenty-something woman, balancing a business career with her role as mom and wife. She was looking for a "sounding board and for wise counsel," she said, but then added, "My generation doesn't have much time for *authority figures*. Rather, what we are looking for is *wisdom figures*."

April spoke for many in our day who have grown weary with and suspicious of authority figures—charismatic preachers, church power players, PhDs, politicians, CEOs, and basically anyone flashing institutional credentials. And this new generation is not afraid to say so. This does not mean, of course, that April and her peers lack God-hunger. In fact, a good many people in our time remain very much open to the supernatural; but at the same time they often express cynicism toward the agents or promoters of "organized religion."

April underscores the bias of this book, that a spiritual leader is not necessarily the person with the most Bible knowledge (though Bible knowledge is of utmost importance), nor the one with the best track record of managerial and administrative skills. It may not even be the person with the strongest leadership skills (at least, as our culture defines leadership). Rather:

A spiritual leader is the kind of person God-hungry people want to be like.

While you will see the preceding words repeated like a mantra throughout this book, they are no mere slogan. Rather, they represent my attempt to encapsulate the DNA at the heart of authentic spiritual leadership. It can help a Christian leader, of course, to know Scripture and to have experience in ministerial skills like teaching, counseling, or facilitating small groups—even in visionary leadership. But by themselves, these skills do not attract God-hungry followers and shape Christ-like lives.

In fact, I suspect that today's so-called "postmodern people" are not so different from most people throughout history. Way back in "Bible times," Scripture declared that what a spiritual leader *is* tends to shape the flock much more than what that leader *claims to believe.* "Remember your leaders, who spoke the word of God to you. Consider the *outcome of their way of life and imitate their faith.*"[2] Note: the emphasis falls not on credentials or expertise, but on character and on how well the leaders navigate their own lives.

A spiritual leader is the kind of person God-hungry people want to be like.

Especially in this way, spiritual leadership differs from all other kinds of leadership. Contrast spiritual leadership with, say, leadership in the practice of medicine. A medical doctor may take years to learn the principles of healthy living: balanced diet, proper exercise, and ample rest, and thus become equipped to train students how to lead a sick person to health—even if the doctor practices none of the healthy disciplines himself and, indeed, possibly even while the doctor grows sicker and sicker. Not so with spiritual leadership, however! Especially in our skeptical, postmodern world.

God-hungry persons are not saying, "Tell me your answers!" But they are urging, "Share your life with me. Let me see it. Are you a person of integrity, of real character? Is your faith 'working' for you? Is the church you lead an authentic community?" God-hungry people want to know the hearts of their shepherds.

SHOW ME YOUR HEART

Hearts matter.

My wife, Carolyn, knows shepherding. She is a consummate spiritual shepherd herself as well as a perceptive observer of shepherds. She writes, "When I look back in my own life to those who had a part in shaping who I am, I remember Elaine Burton, a Sunday-school teacher in the little Tupelo, Arkansas, country church when I was just a child."

Elaine has surfaced in so many of our conversations that one day I asked Carolyn, "Tell me some of the things Elaine Burton taught you." Carolyn sat quietly awhile. I think I could see her eyes peering into the long ago. Finally, she answered a bit wistfully, "Well, I don't actually remember any specific things she taught. I just remember *how she was!*"

Eddie knows shepherds too.

A circle of ministers sat one afternoon, awkwardly reflecting on our pulpit loneliness and confessing our sense of inadequacy. One man in that circle was Eddie Sharp, minister of a large church in our city. Eddie's father also sat in our circle—silent, listening. "Sharp Sr." has been in ministry all of his adult life and has two minister sons. A lot of people know him only as "Eddie's Dad." His own ministry has occurred in small churches. Most of these churches he left better than he found them; some he left sooner than he would have wished, usually with tears but never with bitterness.

In our circle that day, Eddie sent warm tears rolling down his father's cheeks as Sharp Jr. recalled, "Here sits the man who has made the difference for me. I don't remember much about his sermons. I just remember what kind of man he was."

Tears bathed my cheeks too.

Elaine and Eddie's dad both have the heart of a shepherd.

Yes! Oh, yes, at the end of the day, the heart is what matters most to God-hungry people. And to God.

one: THE HEART OF THE MATTER

HEARTS MATTER TO GOD

When God sent Samuel out to find a man fit to lead God's people, Samuel pondered hearts. Saul, the first king, had held so much promise. He so *looked* the part—but he didn't have the heart.

So God sent Samuel in search of someone better. Still, when Samuel met the sons of Jesse, who first caught the prophet's eye? Eliab, the tall and impressive looking one—that is, until God reminded Samuel,

> Do not consider his appearance or his height,
>> for I have rejected him.
>>> The LORD does not look at the things man looks at.
> Man looks at the outward appearance,
>> but *the LORD looks at the heart.*[3]

God had His eye on the shepherd boy who had the right quality of heart! But even after Saul anointed David, God sent David back to the pastures to season the young man's heart for the throne. The psalmist explained,

> He chose David his servant. . . .
>> From tending the sheep he brought him
>>> to be the shepherd of his people. . . .
> And David shepherded them with *integrity of heart.*"[4]

Integrity of *heart.* Don't miss that! In fact, God himself calls David a man after *his own heart.*[5] The Shepherd-King David had a heart hungry for God. Listen to him pray:

> My *heart* says of you "Seek his face!"
>> Your face, LORD, I will seek.[6]

> May the words of my mouth and the *meditation of my heart*
>> be pleasing in your sight,
>>> O LORD, my Rock and my Redeemer.[7]

Create in me a *pure heart*, O God,

and renew a steadfast spirit within me.[8]

This notion will never become outdated. The wind can never whisk it away and cause it to be forgotten. Long after Samuel's day, for example, Isaiah the prophet put his finger on the folly of correct religious words without an authentic heart for God when he lamented, "These people come near to me with their mouth, but *their hearts are far from me*."[9] Seven centuries later, Jesus repeated Isaiah's words, setting the "heart of the matter" in stone for all time.

AND WHAT IS "THE HEART"?

What precisely do we mean by "the heart"? Of course, in Scripture, the term usually does not refer to the literal blood pump. Rather, it is a metaphor for something infinitely larger and deeper.

Some say the heart refers primarily to the brain and the central nervous system; thus, growing a heart for God would be to program the mind with God thoughts and condition the central nervous system to godly reflexes.

Others equate the heart more with the emotions. So we often hear statements like, "My religion moved down twelve inches, from my head to my heart."

I believe a biblical view of "the heart" includes all of the above—plus a whole lot more, much of which defies human understanding. Attempting a precise technical definition thus runs the risk of "mechanizing" the mystery of the human being. So I won't go there. I'll say only that, taken all together, Scripture seems to refer to "the heart" of a person as one's core character, which goes beyond mind and emotions and will to the deepest motivations and passions that drive his or her life. That, at least, is my assumption in this book.

Surely, the heart of the shepherd is the heart of the shepherding matter.

one: THE HEART OF THE MATTER

A HEART SEEKING THE FACE OF GOD

How, then, does an aspiring shepherd find this kind of heart? If I am to become "the kind of person God-hungry people want to be like," first and above all *I must eagerly seek the face of God.*

Listen to the prayers of some ancient God-hungry poets:

As the deer pants for streams of water,
    so my soul pants for you, O God.
My soul thirsts for God, for the living God.
    When can I go and meet with God?[10]

And again,

My soul finds rest in God alone;
    my salvation comes from him.
He alone is my rock and my salvation;
    he is my fortress, I will never be shaken.[11]

And yet again,

O God, you are my God,
    earnestly I seek you;
        my soul thirsts for you,
my body longs for you,
    in a dry and weary land
        where there is no water.[12]

Again,

My heart and my flesh cry out for the living God.[13]

And once again,

One thing I ask of the LORD, this is what I seek: . . . to gaze upon the beauty of the LORD.[14]

Jesus summed up this God-hunger in a blessing that contained a promise: "Blessed are those who hunger and thirst for righteousness, for they will be filled."[15] Hunger for God will not starve one to death, but to life!

Across the centuries since biblical days, the greatest spiritual leaders have always hungered for God. St. Augustine captured God-hunger in his classic phrase, "You made us for yourself, O Lord, and our hearts are restless until they find their rest in you." Still later John Wesley made it clear that shepherds must make an intimate friendship with God their first concern. When ordaining a lay leader, Wesley raised three fundamental questions: "Does he know God? Does he desire and seek nothing but God? Has he the love of God abiding in him?"[16]

This is the kind of heart, even today, that both God and God-hungry people are looking for.

THE WAY OF THE HEART

We cannot lead people where we have not gone. When we merely talk a religious game without God-hungry hearts—even if we tell our people true words—we betray them at the deepest level. Either consciously or subconsciously, we lead our people down the same misguided path into which we ourselves have strayed. We lead them toward the shallows, rather than deeper into the heart of God. More importantly, we betray the trust of our heavenly Father and dishonor his magnificent name.

The good news, however, is that the heart of every helpful shepherd provides a dwelling place for the Good Shepherd. And the soul of a spiritual shepherd still cries out, "Search me, O God, and *know my heart*. . . . See if there is any offensive way in me, and lead me in the way everlasting."[17]

So walk with me through these pages and together let us explore *the heart of a shepherd.*

CARDIOVASCULAR WORKOUTS
FOR SHEPHERD HEARTS

John Wesley used the following set of questions in peer accountability groups. You might find them valuable as you offer self-examining prayers before God. Get out a pen and make yourself some notes. Prayerfully ask yourself each of these questions, and then write down your answers. Finally, pray over your answers.

1. Is the love of God shed abroad in my heart?

2. Does any sin, inward or outward, have dominion over me?

3. Do I really desire that others tell me what they think, fear, and hear concerning me?

4. Have I mentioned any failing or fault of any person when it was unnecessary to do so?

5. Have I unnecessarily grieved anyone by word or deed?

6. Have I desired the praise of men?

7. Have I resumed my claim to my body, soul, friends, fame, or fortune, which I gave over to God?

8. Have I said anything with a stern look, accent, or gesture, particularly regarding religion?[18]

*The chief end of man is to glorify
God and enjoy him forever.*

—Westminster Shorter Catechism

two

A HEART COMPELLED BY THE GLORY OF GOD

We were chosen . . . that we might be . . . for the praise of his glory.

—Paul the Apostle

The man who ran the motor pool at the university where I taught as an adjunct professor, "Sam," once told me, "Doctor Lynn, I think I have been called to preach."

"And why do you think so?" I asked.

"Well," he replied with a wry grin, "I love fried chicken, and I hate work!"

Sam set me thinking about legitimate motives for spiritual leadership. For years I began my semester by asking my ministry students, "Why do you want to be Christian leaders?" Listen to some of their answers:

- "I've got to make a living somehow. And ministry is an honorable profession."

- "I'm good at public speaking, and my parents think I'm cut out for the ministry."

- "I want to be loved and appreciated for doing something worthwhile."

- "It would be very fulfilling to make a difference in the world."

- "I love people."

- "The need is great. The world is lost. Someone must do something."

- "I don't want my life to count for nothing."

And on and on it went. Motives for ministry run the gamut, often a mixture of altruism and self-interest. I certainly understand this, because my own motives slide up and down the "nobility scale" as well. I suspect that if you have attempted any kind of spiritual leadership for very long, your motives have run the gamut too.

ANGER AND GREED

Henri Nouwen once observed that much ministry is marked by anger and greed.[1] At first I thought this comment preposterous! But time has taught me that Nouwen might be right on target.

Greed? Not necessarily greed for money—but maybe for attention or respect or for feelings of well-being and self-worth and fulfillment. Sometimes it's greed to be doing something worthwhile in order to receive spiritual blessings. And yes, even (get this) *greed to go to heaven!* You've heard people say something like, "The most important thing in the world to me is to go to heaven when I die."

Of course, I see nothing wrong with many of these altruistic motives *in themselves*. But there is something dreadfully wrong in them *by themselves*. Even going to heaven is more of a by-product than a goal. In fact, there is a way of desiring heaven that is actually selfish: "I'll get my skinny little backside through the pearly gates, devil take the hind-most." The ultimate example of a selfish view of heaven may be a fanatically religious person who believes that a suicidal act of terrorism earns immediate entrance into heaven. I suppose the last thing passing through the minds of the terrorists who slammed the airliners into the World Trade Center could have been, "I get to go to heaven now."

It is not the *pearly gates*, however, but the *presence of God* that makes heaven appealing. If we do not relish the presence of God, here and now, then heaven forever would be a drag. The reward for serving God is getting more of God himself.

Do you know why I married Carolyn? I married her because I wanted her. I didn't marry her to get a house that she might bring to the marriage. The chief reward in marrying Carolyn is to get more of her, not to share in her possessions. Just so, the reward of seeking God is not a place, but a presence. Let me repeat: the reward for serving God is getting more of God himself.

And what about the anger? When people don't help us fulfill our greed (in our perception), when they respond poorly or they perform badly or won't cooperate with us or appreciate us, we might be tempted to feel angry toward them. Why? Because they are not helping us feel good about ourselves.

But sooner or later the blame may turn inward toward our own sense of inadequacy. "I'm no good at this." "I don't pray enough." "I'm too lazy." "I'm sinful." Or some other ill-identified issues. Maybe my poor results mean I am not a faithful Christian, so how can I be sure I will go to heaven when I die? When we don't match up to our own expectations, we become angry at ourselves and internal anger seethes.

But that's not all.

GUILT

In not a few would-be spiritual leaders, the anger eventually identifies *God* as the culprit. "*He* is the one who cooked up this whole system—

and it doesn't work. He is the one who sucked me into it—and then doesn't deliver according to my expectations."

Then follows the guilt: "How can I let myself become so bitter toward people whom I am supposed to love?" And, horror of horrors, "Will lightning strike me because I feel angry at the Almighty?" Guilt stirred with anger becomes a toxic brew.

Oh, yes! Nouwen *is* onto something: when we minister out of skewed motives, greed and anger and guilt feed one another.

What has happened in such cases? What goes awry with our good intentions? Maybe we have not worked the list of motives far enough. We may have settled for some motives that may or may not be bad *in themselves*, but *taken by themselves*, are profoundly inadequate and so cannot help but fail us. Our hearts have not come to the central and undergirding motive that keeps a person in joyful service for a lifetime, no matter what.

"Ah, yes," you may be asking, "and what is this central and undergirding motive?"

HEART OF THE MOTIVE: GOD'S GLORY

The Westminster Shorter Catechism declares, "The chief end of man is to glorify God and enjoy him forever." This is true and right on the mark, not merely because it is in the catechism, but because it is in the Bible! It is also written into the book of human nature: God-hungry people want to be like a person who has the heart to seek and glorify God.

In the book of Ephesians, the apostle Paul underscores God's glory as this central and undergirding motive. The ancient Greek language did not have punctuation marks and font changes to highlight key points. Rather, to emphasize an important point, a writer in ancient Greek times repeated his point frequently in close succession. And here in Ephesians 1, Paul repeats his "important point" three times in one Greek sentence. Notice:

> He chose us in him before the creation of the world
>> to be holy and blameless . . .
>>> to the *praise of his glorious grace.*

> In him we [Gentiles] were also chosen . . .
>> in order that we . . . might be
>>> for the *praise of his glory.*

> [And He sealed us with] . . . the promised Holy Spirit . . .
>> *to the praise of his glory.*[2]

(Although the English Bible breaks up this section into several sentences, in the Greek it appears all as one long sentence.)

Paul makes his point clear: The glory of God is the focus of life, which means the nature of God is the central motive for ministry. Glorifying God is the *only* motive that survives the grueling and draining challenges of spiritual service—especially spiritual leadership—over the long haul.

The apostle seems still to be basking in this glory two chapters later when he bursts out, "To him be glory in the church and in Christ Jesus throughout all generations, for ever and ever! Amen."[3] Yes, the apostle indeed affirms that "glorifying God and enjoying him forever" is not only the core motive for Christian service; it is the central point of human existence itself!

This idea wasn't new to Paul, of course, nor is it by any means confined to this single text. Rather, in this one glorious sentence the apostle touches on a dominant theme running through the whole Bible. When our hearts begin to long for the glory of God, our eyes begin to see it in nearly every chapter. From the very beginning, God Himself longed for his glory to be reflected in these human beings he so much loved. The chief end of man has *always* been to "glorify God and enjoy him forever."

THE FACE OF GLORY

"But," you ask, "what is glory?"

Attempting to define "glory" is as elusive as trying to define God. All definitions fall far short. But one of the better attempts came from first-century rabbis who called it *Shekinah*. For the ancient rabbis, Shekinah glory meant all of the combined attributes of God, distilled in unrefracted, blazing, glorious light. Shekinah glory! This glorious light was irresistible, and yet at the same time, unapproachable upon pain of death.

This is the kind of glory emblazoned across the pages of the Bible. When God called Moses to lead His people out of Egypt, for example, "Moses said to the LORD, 'You have been telling me, "Lead these people," but you have not let me know whom you will send with me.'"

God assured Moses, "My Presence will go with you."[4]

But Moses persisted and finally spit out what he really had in mind: "Now *show me your glory*."[5]

Let me give you Anderson's New Free Translation of God's response. "Then God said to Moses, 'Son, you're not wired for *that*. Why, if I were to give you a full frontal view of my glory, it would crash your hard drive. Besides, I am God and you aren't—and I will not explain myself to you. Just trust me, Son.

"'Now, here is what I *will* do: I will put you in a rocky crevice, cover you with my hand, and my glory will pass by. Afterward I will take my hand away and let you look at the afterglow.'"[6]

So Moses got to see "afterglow," nothing more. Yet even the *tracks* of God's glory so overwhelmed Moses with their majesty that his face lit up like a neon light. In fact, Moses's face shone so brightly that when he came back to the people, he had to put a sack over his head to keep from frightening the Israelites out of their wits. So Moses let "the Glory" seep out a little at a time, at a level the people could handle. And when "the Glory" began to dissipate completely, he would go back into "the Presence," pull the sack off his head, and get his face all "gloried up" again.[7]

Note, however, that Moses couldn't stay too long in either place. If he stayed too long with the people, he eventually had no glory to reflect. He had to go back into the Presence. But if he stayed only in the Presence, he was of no value to the people. So his ministry reflected a rhythm of worship and service: "the people" and "the Presence." *Approaching* God's glory and *reflecting* God's glory. What a compelling metaphor for Christian leadership! Rhythm between the mountain and the masses, between receiving and reflecting God's glory.

Moses glorified God the same way the moon glorifies the sun. The moon has no glory of its own. Without the sun, the moon is nothing but a sterile ball of dirt. But when it gets positioned to reflect the sun's glory into our world—and that's all it does—the moon covers us with a silver magic.

Today's spiritual shepherds glorify God in precisely the same way, by reflecting God's glory. We shepherds have no glory of our own. We cannot add to God's glory. But if we come regularly before him, our faces get "gloried up" and we can reflect his glory into our world. We glorify God by finding a rhythm between seeking his face and reflecting his glory into the lives of people around us.

At the heart of a shepherd lies a hunger for God's glory. From the face of such a shepherd beams the reflection of God's glory, and from the hands and the lips of such a shepherd flow the quality of service and grace that demonstrates God's glory, even in the midst of the most ordinary circumstances. Put simply: we glorify God best by treating people the way God treats people—with grace, mercy, love, and encouragement.

DRIVEN BY GLORY

Even the dullest eye cannot miss God's glory in the call of the Old Testament prophets. For them, ministry was not merely an exercise of human giftedness or longing for personal or religious fulfillment, not even refined altruism. Rather, the prophets ministered to the glory of God!

Witness Isaiah, for example: "I saw the Lord seated on a throne, high and exalted." The flying seraphim shouted, "Holy, holy, holy is the LORD Almighty; the whole earth is full of his *glory*." In the midst of this earthshaking, soul-shattering encounter with the Almighty, Isaiah's personal aspirations came unraveled. Isaiah himself comprehended his own "unravel-ment" and sensed the "undone-ness" all around him in his world full of "unclean lips."[8]

Only after God's purifying, red-hot coal had touched Isaiah's lips could our awestruck friend hear the call of God—and only then could the prophet respond. But again, note carefully: he responded to the glory of God. He did not respond to the clamor of human need or to some inner longing to earn self-worth, but to the awesome glory of the Holy One.

Both the true motive and the true measure of ministry issue from the nature of God.

Ray Anderson states this almost like a riddle: "Ministry is to God on behalf of people, not people on behalf of God."[9] Otherwise, contends Anderson, God's ministry often falls prey to mere pragmatism and utilitarianism and winds up being measured by "what works" and "what people think they need" rather than in terms of the will and the glory of God. And when the "results" don't seem obvious—or don't measure up to our expectations—burnout lurks not too far down the road.

When the glory of God is the measure of a shepherd's Christian service and leadership, however, then discouragement and disillusionment present less serious threats to the shepherd—even to one who feels very ordinary.

God did not cut his orders for Isaiah contingent on results through human effort or human responsiveness. In fact, God armed Isaiah with such a dangerous message that it would actually damage human hearts if they rejected it. Besides, strangely, God even told Isaiah that the people would not listen! To top it off, when Isaiah asked how long he should stay on this futile-sounding assignment, God told him to stay and preach "until the houses are left deserted and the fields ruined and ravaged" and everyone has gone away.[10]

> Both the true motive and the true measure of ministry issue from the nature of God.

From a purely human perspective, Isaiah's mission seems like an exercise in futility. But at the very heart of Isaiah's motivation, God planted the ever-active antidote to discouragement, bitterness, and disillusionment. Isaiah did not minister primarily to man on behalf of God, but to God on behalf of man. God wanted Isaiah to *faithfully reflect God's glory*, regardless of his "success."

We cannot "fix" people nor can we "make them respond." And so long as Isaiah—and you and I—understand that God's glory is the *object of*, the *motive for*, and the *measure of* ministry, we will never have lasting cause for despair over our lack of "results."

After all, how can a person ever burn out on the glory of God? Soft motives sap our nerve, but solid motives feed strong courage.

So is this an excuse for laziness or careless methods? Of course not. These do not glorify God, either. But this does mean that the glory of God is the only motive that keeps us going for a lifetime.

If love of bringing glory to God does not top one's list of motives, overriding and undergirding every other motive, a would-be spiritual leader will not likely stick to the task. And even so far as he or she does hang in, it will mostly be with a plodding, wooden, unattractive kind of doggedness that people can smell a mile off—and that repels those hungry for God.

GLORY LOST-AND-FOUND

When God's people took their land and built God's house, God flooded the temple with his unapproachable glory.[11] But people abused the temple, so "the glory departed" and the sad word *Ichabod* rent the air: "God's glory is gone."[12] Yet even though God took his glory from a rebellious people, he gave the prophets rough sketches of his future "glory" plans. So they wrote things like this:

> "Here is my servant, whom I uphold,
>> my chosen one in whom I delight;
>>> I will put my Spirit on him. . . .
> He will not shout or cry out,
>> Or raise his voice in the streets.
>>> A bruised reed he will not break.[13]

Tell me, prophet—who is this One that brings justice with gentleness? Tell me more.

> He was despised and rejected . . .
>> Like one from whom men hide their faces.[14]

Oh, now the picture grows clearer:

> He was pierced for our transgressions,
>> he was crushed for our iniquities;
>>> the punishment that brought us peace was upon him,
> and by his wounds we are healed.[15]

Now, God, I am beginning to see you set the whole stage of history for the dramatic entry of your glorious Messiah into our world.

GLORY WITH SKIN ON

The apostle John spelled out the ultimate glory headlines: "The Word became flesh and made his dwelling among us. We have seen his glory, the glory of the One and Only, who came from the Father, full of grace and truth."[16]

The glory that once dwelt in light unapproachable and upon pain of death; the glory that was with God before calendars and beyond space, when he dreamed his dream in cosmic darkness; that glory and that word are combined in the flesh that chose to walk like us. "Dwelt" among us! Pitched his shepherd's tent in our pasture!

And he did not come "to be served, but to serve, and to give his life as a ransom for many."[17] For Jesus, to glorify God was to serve people—and ultimately lay down His life for them.

And here is the truly astounding part: the glory of God made flesh in Jesus *can now be reflected in us.* We, the church, are now the body of Christ in our world.[18] "And we, who with unveiled faces all *reflect the Lord's glory*, are being transformed into his likeness with ever-increasing glory, which comes from the Lord, who is the Spirit."[19] So John concludes, "No one has ever seen God; but if we love one another, God lives in us and his love is made complete in us."[20] In other words, people see God's glory reflected in us when we treat people like Jesus treats people—that is, when we serve them, even lay down our lives for them.

Shepherds compelled by the glory of God will far more likely stay the course. His glory will illumine their faces and gild their tracks—and draw the trust of God-hungry persons who want to be like such shepherds.

Now flip back to Ephesians, and find the third chapter for Paul's "glory finale." These kinds of shepherds will be "strengthened with might by his Spirit in the inner man," and "Christ will live in their hearts" and they will be "filled with all the fullness of God." And in the end they will accomplish "more than they could have asked or imagined."[21] It is then that the glory of God breaks out in the Christian community, which is "his body." And so Paul leads us in praise: "To him be *glory in the church* and in Christ Jesus throughout all generations, for ever and ever! Amen."[22]

So I ask again: why do you want to be a Christian leader? Why attempt to shepherd God's people?

The compelling, undergirding, and long-lasting motive in the heart of an authentic shepherd is "to glorify God and enjoy Him forever."

No other motive is enough!

CARDIOVASCULAR WORKOUTS
FOR SHEPHERD HEARTS

Reality check below: What drives you? What may need to change?

Work your way down both columns, and jot down examples of when your motives may have been shame-based or God-directed.

(Note: the "shame" referred to here is not guilt over a real sin. Rather, it is a vague feeling of unworthiness, badness, or guilt unattached to a specific, sinful action.)

SHAME-BASED VS. GOD-DIRECTED SERVICE	
Sanctified Co-dependency *(Self-Protective Manipulation)*	Compassionate Service *(Christ-Centered Ministry)*
Motivated by self-protection and energized by self-effort.	Motivated and energized by the Holy Spirit of God.
Characterized by legalistic and joyless works.	Characterized by a sense of peace and purpose.
People become statistics or projects to be "won" or "fixed."	People are seen as being the same as I; need to be lovingly led to Jesus Christ as Savior and "fixer."
I enjoy serving most when the task is a monumentally big deal.	I enjoy all service to which Christ calls me, even if it appears small.
I demand external validation through public attention and appreciation and become resentful if I go unnoticed.	I can accept attention, but I don't demand it; I can remain unnoticed without growing resentful.
Serving is a source of my identity and sense of worth in the church.	My service is the outgrowth of an identity based on being a loved, redeemed bearer of God's image.
In the name of "Christian love," I bail out others, not expecting them to take personal responsibility for themselves.	I take responsibility for myself under Christ's lordship and let go of others to do the same.
I jump in and take care of others without waiting to be asked.	I give help appropriately when asked (emergencies excepted).
As the "server," I feel and appear competent and powerful (like a savior). The "servee" feels and appears incompetent and weak (like a victim).	"Server" and "servee" have attitudes of mutual respect whereby neither feels nor appears incompetent, for we both realize our roles might be reversed next time.
I use my busyness for God to numb painful feelings and distract me from unmanageable parts of my life.	My active serving is balanced with quiet times of prayer, Bible study, and meditation on Scripture when I reflect on my total lifestyle.
I often feel burned out and bitter because I don't take care of my health and I'm unable to set limits.	I can say no to requests of others for I recognize my own limitations and need for healthy self-care.[23]

I had come into the parish seeing its great potential as a learning center, a kind of mini-university in which I was the resident professor. And then one day, in a kind of shock of recognition, I saw that it was in fact a worship center. . . . Out of that recognition a conviction grew: that my primary educational task as pastor was to teach people to pray.

—Eugene H. Peterson, *The Comtemplative Pastor*

three

A HEART ON ITS KNEES

I pray that out of his glorious riches he may strengthen you with power through his Spirit in your inner being.

—Ephesians 3:16

On a snowy night in February of 2003, some friends and I drove through the hills of Tennessee to the home of Albert and Patsy. Albert's ministry of prayer had breathed fresh life into this 173-year-old church. So it was appropriate that this special prayer meeting be in his house.

A woman from Ohio had heard about "the praying shepherds" at this church and how they regularly prayed over people and anointed them with oil in the spirit of James 5:14. So she had driven her daughter from Ohio, seeking prayer. Her daughter had a promising future as one of the top female high-school athletes in the state of Ohio. Several weeks earlier, however, doctors had diagnosed her with MS. "Your track career is over," she learned.

After some food and pleasantries, a loving, silver-haired shepherd of the church knelt before the young lady, quietly opened his Bible, and began reading—no, praying—the Twenty-Third Psalm. He then took a vial of oil from his pocket and gently anointed the young girl's forehead. Then he held her and cried out to God for her peace and her health.

We drove back to our lodging surrounded by darkness and falling snow, but with a sense of warmth and light in our spirits. We felt that even if God should not heal the young woman's body, a good deal of soul-healing had taken place that night. "And that in itself would have been enough for us," the girl and her mother said.

As a postscript: that young lady from Ohio is now a sophomore in a Christian university, and with only one minor setback is enjoying full mobility. She's pursuing her studies—and track.

That night in Albert and Patsy's house was not unusual, however. This kind of pastoral prayer happens several times a week in that church, for each shepherd has "a heart on its knees."

AN EMERGING PATTERN

Recently, as we drove away from yet another weekend of consulting with church leaders, a friend rolled out the old, tired line, "I think we are seeing a pattern here."

"And the pattern is?" I probed.

"It's clear as day: The shepherds who have hearts for prayer—the ones who really do spend a lot of time on their knees—are the ones that people want to follow. They are also the ones God seems to be using to really change lives."

"Yes," I had to agree, "I see that pattern too."

My friend Rick Atchley helps explain why this is true: "Our sovereign God often makes the sovereign choice to accomplish his will only when asked to do so. Some of God's promises don't happen because no one asked God for them to happen."[1]

I think Rick may be on to something here.

Peter says, for example, that the Lord is "not wanting anyone to perish" and that he wants everyone "to come to repentance."[2] Yet not everyone repents and many will perish. Just because something is God's will doesn't mean it will happen.

Think about this. Jesus taught us to pray, "Your kingdom come, your will be done on earth as it is in heaven."[3] Surely he wants his kingdom to come; yet he taught us to pray for it. Could the kingdom seem to be so slow in coming because God's people are so anemically praying for it to come? In fact, "Your Father knows what you need before you ask him,"[4] but he does not promise to give it until we ask him.

God is clearly willing to do many things he will not necessarily do until we ask him.

It is when you "ask," Jesus says, that "it will be given to you."[5] As Atchley further observes, "Shepherds must learn to pray, 'God, do what you said you would do.' Strangely, we preach sermons and sing songs about our confidence that God was active in real time in the past and that he will also act mightily in the future. Why, then, should we have a problem believing God is really active in the present?"[6]

WHEN SHEPHERDS PRAY

Good shepherds ask all the time, expecting answers, that God will heal sick bodies, sick marriages, and broken lives, and unleash his power in our churches and our communities today. The exciting thing about a mighty God is not how powerful God was, but how powerful he is. His name is "I AM," not "I was." Again Atchley comments: "God is alive and active so He will not stay put. History is not written in stone—God longs to change things. We need not believe that things must stay the way they are!"

The Bible says that God is "able to do immeasurably more than all we ask or imagine, according to his power that is at work within us."[7] As someone said, "Nothing lies outside the reach of prayer except what lies outside the will of God."

I agree with Rick: "Dear shepherds, in your church, things are likely going to stay the same until God gets you out of your meetings and onto your knees. True, prayer can be hard work. Paul said, 'I urge you, brothers . . . to join me in my struggle by praying to God.'[8] He even called this prayer thing 'wrestling' or 'agonizing.'[9] We are likely not really praying 'apostle style' if our praying is not work."[10]

Haddon Robinson puts it this way: "The work is prayer. Ministry is the reward for the work."

LEADING FROM OUR KNEES

Again, Rick Atchley says, "God likely will not empower shepherds whose meetings consist of two minutes of 'agonizing' and three hours of 'organizing' (two minutes of prayer, three hours of talk)." Today, too, the best shepherds of God's people model the priority of prayer in the midst of the fray. Not as a last resort, but as the first step. Rick calls this "leading through pleading."[11]

Just one simple example of this: David Davenport, former president of Pepperdine University, wrote to me, "One favorite shepherding story . . . As a young minister I had a call in the middle of the night that one of our church family had died and that the loved ones wanted me to come to the hospital. I called one of the elders, who got up in the middle of the night to go with me. By the time we arrived at the hospital, he had concluded that because of some difficult family/church situations, it might be off-putting for him to go in with me. So he prayed with and for me—and them—and waited for me in the car. I felt very much affirmed and supported that he would get up in the night and, out of sensitivity to all of us, just sit in the car and pray in support."

That shepherd was leading by pleading.

In an "elders meeting," the shepherds at a large church were asked, "Let's see a show of hands of those who pray daily for our church." The shepherds felt embarrassed and chagrined at how few of them did. "At that moment," they later recalled, "we woke up from a long, dark night. For years we had been meeting on long, laborious agendas about attendance, contributions, keeping people happy, real-estate acquisitions—some meetings lasting till one in the morning. We had prayed very little; basically just brief opening and closing prayers."

But God began to change their role that day. Now these shepherds say, "Let others do the administration and management. We want to pray for the people and want to be with the people." Some years have passed since these pivotal moments, and now they say, "When we meet monthly, it is to pray about people. Or to be with people. Most of the time we used to spend meeting, we now spend with people, praying with people, shepherding people."

Amazing things began to happen in that church. Within three or four years, some thirty marriages that had been in separation or even divorce came back together.

Evangelism also began to flourish. The shepherds led and the church followed, simply seeking God's will in prayer and asking for God's power. Teams of people walk through the sanctuary during the week praying for God to "bring people to this pew—and to that one." In the following three years, that church baptized more than four hundred people.

FUELED BY THE SPIRIT

But listen further. By all means, don't miss the connection between prayer and the real-time power of the Holy Spirit in our shepherding hearts. Among Paul's many prayers for the people he loved, this one stands out for me: "I pray that out of his glorious riches he may strengthen you with power through his Spirit in your inner being."[12]

Think of it: Prayer actually releases the power of the Holy Spirit within us! We are "strengthened" in our inner persons. Yes, God answers our prayers that he use his power to change lives.

What is more, on a very practical level, he supplies physical, emotional, and spiritual energy to weary shepherds, through the indwelling of his Holy Spirit.

This past summer as my wife, Carolyn, was leading a group of pastor's wives in an interdenominational retreat, she pointed them to 1 Peter 4:11: "If anyone serves . . . do it with the strength God provides."

> We have been able to persevere only in "the strength that God provides."

The passage rang bells. One woman acknowledged that she had never noticed it before—or at least had never zip-coded it to her own life. But if this single verse was all she took home, she said, the whole retreat was worth it.

Carolyn and I understand why she would say such a thing. We thank God every day for the privilege of shepherding people. We love it. Always have. But to be honest, at times the emotional and spiritual drain, the expectations, and the sheer pace have drained us way below "empty." And like most shepherds, we can't count the blue Mondays that found us mentally drafting a resignation, ready to throw in the towel or run screaming into the woods. But somehow, God has given us the strength to hang in.

We certainly don't claim that the strength to hang in comes from any virtue of our own, nor from our rugged constitutions or our stubborn wills. Rather, we have been able to persevere only in "the strength that God provides."

We are not sure of all Peter meant by this ringing challenge to "serve with the strength God supplies." Nor do we understand all of what Paul meant by our being "strengthened with power by his Spirit in the inner being." And we certainly would not compare our trivial struggles with those of first-century believers riding out the storms of persecution.

But Carolyn and I find something quite immediate, personal, and tangible in these words. Whenever we confront demanding assignments, when we cannot seem to muster the energy on our own, we find ourselves turning to Peter's charge to serve with the strength God supplies and Paul's parallel assurance,

> If the Spirit of him who raised Jesus from the dead is living in you,
> he who raised Christ from the dead will also give life to your
> mortal bodies through his Spirit, who lives in you.[13]

Possibly we may draw something more specific from these passages than what the apostles had in mind, but we take them to mean that the Holy Spirit, the one who raised Jesus from the dead, will actually give us the physical vitality and energy to do what God wants done through us at the moment.

GETTING PERSONAL

Carolyn says, "I witnessed God's strength again this past weekend. We headed into another state for a couples retreat. When we left home, Lynn was both sick and exhausted—without energy. On the way, he wondered how he was going to muster the strength and concentration to stand up and teach with any effectiveness. I was praying the 1 Peter 4 and Romans 8 kind of prayers for him: 'life for your mortal bodies' and 'strength that God supplies.'"

"Somehow, God showed up at that retreat," Carolyn told me afterward. "It was as though you stepped out of the way. Your body was there but another force took over. I never heard you teach in a more compelling way. I am sure that others thought it was just 'Lynn way beyond his best.' But I knew the difference. God supplied the energy for his appointed time and place."

Some months earlier, Carolyn had gone for two weeks to Guinea, West Africa—the poorest nation in Africa. When she boarded the plane, she began to wonder what had possessed her to make such a commitment. She asked herself, *What can I do in two weeks to honor God there, much less make any difference?*

She left tired and arrived even further exhausted, and then launched into ten whirlwind days of nonstop, intense, and draining work. "I felt so tired," she remembers, "and I began to pray that God would give me an extra measure of energy."

The villagers saw "that white woman" cleaning chickens for dinner. They also watched her at the clinic, swatting flies from the sores of the patients, and washing faces. Sometimes they observed her walking through the village, holding the cold hands of malaria-infected little girls, or rocking them to sleep in her arms. Maybe they even glimpsed her through a window, washing dishes.

"Of course," Carolyn acknowledges, "I know that I could be running only on 'the strength God supplies.' I also ran on the borrowed credibility of Caitlin, our nineteen-year-old granddaughter, who had been there doing these things for five months before I arrived.

"I watched Caitlin, with medical tweezers, debriding third degree burns on a little girl, while Andress, Caitlin's older sister, stood by to dispose of the dead skin. All the while, 1 Peter 4:11 kept repeating itself in my head. I knew our two granddaughters were able to do this only in 'the strength God supplies.'"

So we look up in prayer for the grace and strength God supplies.

LOOKING UP

Most shepherds of God's flock will find dark valleys on their journey that sap their energy. Frequently you may feel so exhausted that with one more step your knees will buckle. The good news is that the Holy Spirit of the living God promises strength for the way. And Paul says the Holy Spirit's power is released into us through prayer.[14]

Even if a person has the rugged constitution and dogged determination to "hang in"—but without the power of God at work—his or her efforts may prove futile at worst or mechanical and stiff at best, which leaves a bad taste in the mouths of those who easily see through such a charade. In fact, centuries ago the great shepherd poet of God's people reminded us,

Unless the LORD builds the house,
     its builders labor in vain.
Unless the LORD watches over the city,
     the watchmen stand guard in vain.[15]

Love Maria Willis expressed the same sentiment in her 1864 hymn:

Father, hear the prayer we offer, not for ease our prayer shall be,
     But for strength that we may ever live our lives courageously.[16]

God provides strength, through his grace, poured in from above us. My friend Gary is a prime example of a praying shepherd who knows he can carry on only with God's strength.[17] He writes,

One day when I first took on the name "shepherd," driving home from a really tough day at work, I counted twenty-six calls to return to folks from within my flock. I felt so overwhelmed that I pulled over the Jeep and wept uncontrollably. "I can't handle this," I told myself.

When I arrived home, I picked up a little book my son Joshua had sent me. I had shared my feelings of ineptness with him. He had prayed over me, then later sent me this copy of *The Living Reminder*.[18] It tutors shepherds to be "living reminders" of what God is doing for those who are learning to trust His leading. "Our job," insists Nouwen, is "to pray, and serve in the memory of Jesus Christ."

"Even in Jesus's own farewell discourse," Nouwen reminds us, "Jesus said to his disciples, 'It is for your own good that I am going, because unless I go, the [Holy Spirit] will not come to you' (John 16:7, 13). Jesus shows his closest friends that in memory an even more real intimacy with him will be possible. In memory the Holy

Spirit will enable them to experience a fuller meaning of what Jesus is to them."

How freeing this was to me. Now as I meet with folks, I simply share stories. Stories from "The Book" that connect with each specific situation. Stories from the lives of folks from within our church family who have walked through similar situations. We then pray for his guidance for them. As I leave the house, I try to pray inwardly, "It is good that I leave this house." Then aloud, "I leave your Holy Spirit in charge of this couple, family, and home."

It can never be about what I must do for someone, but rather all about what he will do. Now I don't feel so overwhelmed. Only eager to share stories, pray—and *leave*, so His Spirit can get to work![19]

This praying shepherd is the kind of person that God-hungry people want to be like.

Listen up: "The community of faith will always need more people who can pray, but can't lead. But we really don't need any more that lead but don't pray. God moves mountains. Prayer moves God."[20]

May God raise up more shepherds who cry out to him day and night for the flock in their care. Then we will see God's power released within us and among us.

CARDIOVASCULAR WORKOUT FOR SHEPHERD HEARTS

Try one or two options or a combination of both:

Option A: Get with one or two other shepherds you know well and that you trust deeply. Discuss the following questions, one by one, and then pray for each other.

Option B: Carve out at least two hours. Take a notebook and pen with you. Go to a quiet place, and slowly work your way through these questions. Journal your reflections and the commitments you make to yourself. Then keep a journal of prayers and the ways God answers them.

1. What do you think of the statement, "Nothing lies outside the reach of prayer, except what lies outside the will of God"?

2. What great change might God want to bring to your life, but is waiting until you ask for it?

3. What will you claim for your church that only God can deliver?

4. What will you claim for a person in your flock that only God can deliver?

5. Think of something to pray for so huge that only God could get credit for it—and pray for it!

6. What might God need to do in your church for you to regularly go to church thinking, *I don't know what God will do, but when we leave, we will be talking about it?*

Hear my voice when I call, O LORD;
be merciful to me and answer me.

—David, in Psalm 27:7

four

A PRAYER PATH FOR SHEPHERDS

Pray in the Spirit on all occasions.

—Ephesians 6:18

A dozen Christian men leaned in around a table discussing something big: prayer! "I hate to admit it," James confessed, "but sometimes my schedule gets so hectic that for days I don't really pray much."

"I usually pray fairly regularly," Brad joined in. "But my prayers often feel stale, and I get into this rut, praying the same old things every day."

Clark agreed: "I hear that. Rote, stale, and repetitive. Plus, my prayers become narrower and narrower. Here lately I pray mostly about me: my needs, my family, and my ministry. Me!"

James, Brad, and Clark (not their real names) are not mere novices in the faith. They are all widely respected Christian leaders. And, of course, their struggles are not unique. Across the country, lots of sincere shepherds sometimes find themselves stuck in similar ruts:

- Stale and shallow prayers

- Numbing repetition

- Praying mostly about surface issues

- Narrowing scope of prayer topics

- Praying laundry lists of self-centered wants

- Prayer focused on personal wants rather than on relationship with God

- Prayer becoming intermittent, even badly neglected

Sounds both familiar and discouraging, right? So, are these dismal swamps inevitable?

Maybe not.

Most of us who long for more intimacy with God through prayer have tried many prayer formats, habits, postures, formulae, venues, and times. Some we find more helpful than others. Some are merely passing fads. So I always feel reluctant to recommend any approach to you simply because it might seem helpful to me. I do not hesitate, however, to suggest a tried and true pathway to personal prayer renewal that has proven itself to be no mere fad or quick fix. Nevertheless, in our haste to find shortcuts and techniques, we often overlook it. But it is huge.

A BEATEN PATH

For three thousand years virtually all the real giants of the faith—including Jesus—have had one thing in common in their prayer habits:

*They **all** prayed and sang the Psalms!*

Scripture underscores this practice. Surely something larger than coincidence wrote one hundred fifty psalms into the bosom of our Bibles. And it is no mere coincidence that the Psalms flow so freely from the lips of Jesus and the pen of Paul. Nor is it coincidence that those slimmed-down pocket Bibles contain the New Testament plus the Psalms. Nor that, even in our day, believers who long for a deeper walk with God will sooner or later turn to the Psalms.

four: A PRAYER PATH FOR SHEPHERDS

Some of my mentors shepherded me toward praying the Psalms, so for years now the Psalms have lain at the core of my prayer life. They taught me not merely to run through them, but to wallow in them—and most days, to stay there till "God shows up."[1]

THE POINT OF PRAYING PSALMS

During this red-blooded adventure, I have discovered several powerful values of praying the Psalms. Consider just a few of those benefits. Praying the Psalms:

- *helps us speak the unspeakable*—when we have no words for our feelings.

- *helps us explore the uncomfortable*—when we don't want to go to those painful places we need to go.

- *keeps our prayer lists fresh*—by constantly changing the subject.

- *gives strength in weaknesses*—by invoking God's power.

- *takes prayer beyond mere begging*—into praise, adoration, and thankfulness.

- *gets us out of ourselves*—by putting us in touch with the needs and feelings of those around us.

- *gives us a place to belong*—in the long line with three thousand years of God's people who prayed these prayers.

- *helps us thoughtfully process our lives*—by probing into our hearts and raising questions about our motives.

- *gives us resources for ministry*—when the Psalms become tools as we read them into the needs of others.

- *frees us from the myth of certainty*—as they lead us into mystery and paradox and make us comfortable with ambiguity.

- *becomes "leaven" in the flock*—as sheep begin to pray like their shepherds.

- *draws us into encounter with God*—again and again.

I challenge any shepherd to pray five psalms a day for one month. After you have prayed through the Psalter in one month, then beginning in the second month, pray one psalm a day, and continue that pace for the rest of the year. In addition, each month memorize a fresh, key section of one of your favorite psalms.

If you start up this road, however, let me remind you: Don't just read the Psalms. Wallow in them. Stay in each psalm until "God shows up"—whether that takes one minute or two hours.

- Read through your psalm reflectively, slowly, aloud at first.

- Then pray through it carefully—in the first person, making it your own.

- Then pray again, on behalf of others, in the second person.

- And finally, pray the psalm in sheer adoration of God and in surrender to his will.

- Journal your reflections.

Take care not to pray only the psalm. That is, don't end your prayer when the psalm ends. Let the psalm serve as a springboard into the rest of that day's prayers for current issues and persons that the psalm has brought to your heart. Let the psalm shape the day's prayer list.

HANG IN THERE!

If you are like a lot of people, the first few attempts at praying the Psalms may seem to do nothing for you. Don't quit. Stay with it! Trust the process. It takes awhile for the benefits to show. Just as one nutritious meal won't make an undernourished person healthy, neither will one psalm instantly cure "spiritual scurvy."

Again: praying the Psalms is not merely a gimmick or a fad. Great shepherds have traveled this path across the last three thousand years. Even so, this path is not exclusively for an elite corps of contemplative souls. Anyone can walk it—including you. On this path God can awaken, refresh, broaden, and deepen your prayers.

Sure, this prayer journey calls for significant time investment. But it's far more than worth it! Don't knock it till you've tried it. I do not know a single person who has followed this path who ended up disillusioned or even disappointed. God's solution to your prayer problems may actually be this simple, this old, and this obvious.

Blessings to you on the journey.[2]

CARDIOVASCULAR WORKOUTS
FOR SHEPHERD HEARTS

Step One: Pray at least one psalm per day, three times over. (Start with Psalm 1 and work your way through all 150, one per day.)

1. First: read it through aloud, slowly and thoughtfully, to get its sense.

2. Second: pray it aloud slowly, reflectively, in the first person (as your own prayer for yourself). Don't hurry. Wallow in it. Savor it. Mean it.

3. Third: pray it aloud slowly, reflectively, in the second person (as an intercessory prayer on behalf of some other person).

4. Let this psalm springboard you into the rest of your day's prayer.

Step Two: In addition to praying your daily psalm, memorize at least one psalm (or select portion thereof) per month. You can do it! The key is daily repetition.

For memorization:

1. Choose one of your favorite psalms. Choose short ones if you wish. (Or choose sections of long ones, five verses or so.)

2. Break material into small parts, of six to fourteen words, or one to two lines.

3. Do not exceed thirty minutes per day in the first few weeks.

4. Read repetitions aloud, with expression, with your eyes on the words. Then look away to quote repetitions aloud from memory.

5. If you make an error, immediately correct the error four times—aloud.

6. Each day add a few new "small parts" as time allows.

7. Any new "small parts" added from day to day are to be read and quoted, repeated exactly, as the material used on the first day. But material reviewed on day two should be repeated only four times; on day three, repeated three times; on day four, two times. And from the fifth day onward, read and repeated only one time.

A HEART
OF INTEGRITY

And David shepherded them
with integrity of heart.

—Psalm 78:72

five

A HEART IN SEARCH
OF INTEGRITY

*The greatest treason is to do the right
thing for the wrong reason.*
—T. S. Eliot

When J. B. Phillips sat down at his desk before taking on the awesome responsibility of translating the Holy Scriptures from Koine Greek to modern English, he said he felt "something akin to what an electrician might feel if he were rewiring an old house—without the benefit of turning off the mains." Indeed, at times the Bible is so powerful that it can be frightening.

One of the most frightening fragments of Scripture I know is a short verse in John, chapter 5. This verse haunts me, sometimes even awakens me in the night. This convicting verse can nail you like a harpoon in the ribs. Once it penetrates, pulling it out could feel so painful, it might seem easier just to wag it on through life. I have actually been praying that you will walk away from the reading of this chapter, wagging this harpoon on through the rest of your life.

Just a bit of background: Unlike the other three Gospel writers, John makes clear why he wrote his book. He says, "I have written these things so that you might believe."[1] John wrote to produce faith. In the Gospel

53

of John, however, *faith* is never a noun. It is always a verb. *Believing* does not mean merely signing off on a religious idea. Rather, faith is action, allowing Jesus to take one's life in a specific direction.

What is more, John is not trying to produce faith among atheists, nor in the hearts of Buddhists or Muslims or even pagans. Oh, no! John is speaking to religious people—in fact, to some of the church leaders of his day. He wants to produce faith, of all places, among the shepherds!

Remember, Jesus did not get crucified because he was religious. He got crucified because he was dangerous. And the people in most danger were those who had the most vested interest in organized religion— those who got their feelings of significance from climbing up the pecking order of the church or their sense of security from belonging to a stable religious institution. Some even got their very livelihood from the church payroll.

Just before our disturbing verse, John records Jesus as saying, "I know that you do not have the love of God in your hearts."[2] How audacious! Jesus said this to the smartest Bible scholars in town, the most powerful people in the church. But Jesus knew some of them lacked the character to follow new light, because to do so might threaten the very stability and security of their position. And Jesus was definitely "new light"! This is why they hated Jesus so much—and it's what eventually got him crucified.

OK, now—are you ready for the harpoon? Let's read our troubling verse:

> "How can you believe if you accept praise from one another,
>> yet make no effort to obtain the praise
>> that comes from the only God?"[3]

Don't leave this verse too quickly! Read and reread it right now. And think carefully about what Jesus is saying. Note: He did not say, "How can you make it in the system?" Nor, "How can you be popular among the people?" Not even, "How can you feel good about yourself?" Rather, Jesus said, "How can you say that you really believe, if you are driven more by what people think of you than by the glory and honor of God?"

What a piercing question!

Remember, a shepherd of God's people—a spiritual leader—is "the kind of person God-hungry people want to be like." In other words, such an individual is a person of character, a man or woman of integrity to the very marrow of his or her bones.

ALONE IN A CHURCH

As a group of respected Christian leaders sat on the platform one day, I sat among the crowd of anxious church people who fired questions from both right and left. One brash cross-examiner stood and said, "I want to address my question to Reuel Lemmons." (At the time, the late Reuel Lemmons was an entrepreneur, a popular speaker, and the respected editor of a Christian magazine—and because of his homespun style, was widely loved in some Christian circles.) The questioner asked—rather pompously, I thought—"Mr. Lemmons, is it not true that movements which begin as 'freedom in Christ' movements, 'stand-in-front-of-Jesus-with-your-Bible-in-your-hand' movements, movements seeking to pursue God and his truth at all costs . . . is it not true, Mr. Lemmons, that eventually such movements tend to crystallize into institutions, which ultimately wind up persecuting the people who best pursue the original aims of the movement?"

The questioner stood there, waiting, as if he felt Lemmons were responsible for something or other. Then Reuel sauntered to the microphone and in his dry Texas drawl, spoke only one word.

"Yep!"

Then he sat down.

I think Reuel Lemmons was saying something very much like what

Jesus said in John 5: "How can you believe if you accept praise from one another, yet make no effort to obtain the praise that comes from the only God?"

Make no mistake about it: preserving integrity while remaining part of a system is not easy—even if that system is the church that Jesus purchased with his own blood! Nevertheless, real integrity is indispensable to the healthy kind of faith that God-hungry people want to imitate.

Unfortunately, would-be spiritual leaders often feel sorely tempted to dismiss the need for such character, to become more interested in their own prestige or security than in the heart of God and the flock of God. All of us can easily become driven more by the goodwill of our fellows than by our own core convictions. If we go there, however, we not only stunt our own faith development, we also lose credibility as shepherds, as authentic spiritual leaders. God-hungry people do not want to be like a person they do not trust to shoot straight with them. They will place their trust only in a person whose integrity reaches all the way to the core.

FAITH THROUGH STAGES

Let's invite John Westerhoff to help us here. Years back, Westerhoff wrote a seminal, now classic book titled, *Will Our Children Have Faith?*[4] Westerhoff saw faith developing through stages, like the rings of a growing tree.

1. "Experienced" Faith

The first ring in Westerhoff's faith development tree is the "infancy of faith." He calls this "experienced faith." That is, the faith of a little child basically amounts to experiencing the faith of people around him or her, that is, the faith of family and significant others. This is true, whether that faith begins in an infant born into a believing family, or in an unbelieving adult who gets drawn into a community of authentic believers.

2. "Affiliative" Faith

The second, and more crucial, ring in Westerhoff's faith development tree is the "childhood" of faith (which doesn't necessarily coincide with biological childhood). This stage Westerhoff calls "affiliative" faith.

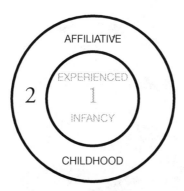

By this, Westerhoff means that in the "affiliative" stage of faith development, a person may be able to tell you what he or she believes. However, these individuals believe what they do primarily because the people with whom they are affiliated believe that sort of thing.

For example, a teenager on a summer mission trip may be able to tell you clearly what his or her church believes about "the plan of salvation," and even spout several related scriptures to "prove" it, but still have little ability to defend or explain it. And as soon as you get such a person off the canned spiel, he or she is immediately in deep weeds—often becoming emphatically more dogmatic and defensive. (Only adolescents become defensive when you get them off their spiel . . . right?)

Of course, the affiliate stage is a normal and healthy part of faith development—provided that one does not get stuck there (more on that later).

For the moment, let's skip to the fourth ring of Westerhoff's faith development tree: the "adulthood" of faith (we will return to ring 3 shortly).

4. "Owned" Faith

Integrity in our hunger for God usually leads ultimately toward a more "mature" or "adult" kind of faith, which Westerhoff calls "owned" faith.

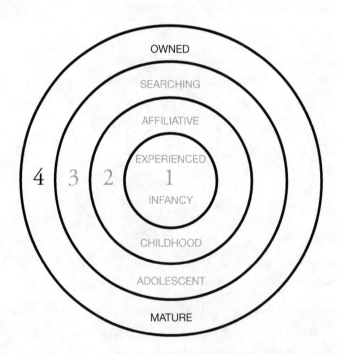

At this more mature stage, a person's faith finds some solid substance. We come to "own" our faith, personally. We own the cost and consequences of our convictions, and we understand a bit more of what we are talking about. This does not mean all our questions have been answered or that all doubts have vanished forever. Neither does it mean that we are completely and consistently living out all of our convictions. It does mean, however, that we have examined and internalized our faith enough so that we can say, "I let my weight down on this." Like the apostle Paul, we say:

> I know whom I have believed, and am convinced that he is able to guard what I have entrusted to him for that day.[5]

This adult, "owned" faith does not look for reputation or power or security. And while this kind of faith holds a deep affection for and loyalty to the community of faith, it will not surrender its own genuine convictions to gain the acceptance and goodwill of the community of faith, just so as to "fit in." Rather, people of mature faith pursue God and his will regardless of where he takes them or what it costs them— even if it disturbs their comfort zones. Even if it radically changes their lifestyles. Even if it calls for great sacrifice. Even if it results in the loss of reputation. This is true "faith of integrity."

3. "Searching" Faith

Now let's return to the ring we skipped. What do we call that transitional period between childhood and adulthood? Adolescence.

Most of us recall how disturbing adolescence can feel. I still remember, at age fourteen or so, feeling afraid to say anything at times, because I did not know which voice would come out of my mouth. Girls wonder, too, when their shape will stop changing—and that makes them feel uncomfortably self-conscious.

Of course, the real change during adolescence is internal. We are trying to discover who we are. We are differentiating ourselves from our parents and becoming free-standing individuals. Consequently, adolescents often seem to challenge almost everything their parents stand for. I remember that sweet, compliant daughter who adored Mom and Dad on Monday, then came out of her room Tuesday all sullen and negative, and did not know any adult with brains—much less Mom and Dad.

This is a frightening time both for the adolescent and for the parents. Wise parents, however, come to see adolescence, with all of its pain and turbulence, as an exciting time—that wondrous season when a child becomes an adult.

Westerhoff says that healthy faith development passes through "faith adolescence" as well. He calls this ring of the faith development tree "searching faith."

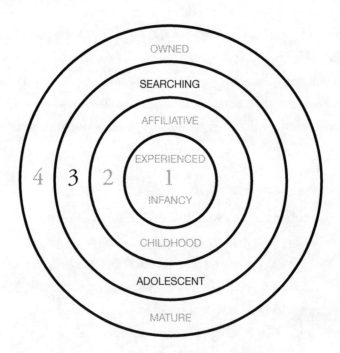

Adolescent (or "searching") faith can occur at any biological age, of course, not necessarily only during junior high. Searching faith becomes unwilling merely to comply. At this stage the God-hungry searcher begins to challenge the presuppositions of affiliative faith, sometimes quite abrasively.

Affiliative church people—men and women whose faith may have stalled at level 2—often feel threatened by these searching questioners. Maybe a searcher pipes up in a Sunday-school class with an off-the-wall, troubling question. "I know that is what you teach, pastor. And yes, I know this is what our denomination believes. But is it really true?" The affiliative believer's neck jerks around, anxiously searching for the questioner, and demands, "Don't you love the church? Are you trying to cause trouble here?" (Chiropractors love these questions; they bring them lots of neck adjustments on Mondays.)

It can also happen at home around the family table: "Mom, Dad—sure, this is what our family believes about the Bible; but my friend Susie and her family read the same Bible every day, and yet they have very different ideas of what it means." In a rigidly affiliative family the parents might respond, "Don't you respect your parents? Why, your grandfather was an elder in our church. Your aunt Rosie was our missionary in Peru!"

Of course, in even the most rigid of homes or churches, people may not actually say these words—but the environment and body language speak just as clearly.

Nevertheless, searching faith, disturbing as it sometimes can feel, is an indispensable stage of faith development. And if someone squelches the searcher's questions, he or she often feels driven toward one of at least three negative options.

First option: Some leave and go down the street to a place that welcomes questions. These days many rigid churches are hemorrhaging in exactly this way. Rigid families too! This is sad for both churches and families. Relationships are strained. Shared memories get lost.

Second option: This gets even more seriously negative. Some with searching questions stay where they are . . . but become angry. You likely know people who can't muster the courage to be openly honest in their search—they fear rejection from their circle of Christian friends or from their church—but at the same time, they cannot ignore their troubling doubts and questions. So they stay put, maybe even staying in some institutional "leadership" role. Inside, however, they seethe with unresolved anger—to the spiritual peril of themselves and everyone around them. I think I know some very religious people, even some church leaders, who have remained angry for decades, leaving a trail of ruptured relationships behind them. This is obviously not a happy option.

Third option: This is more deadly still, yet may be the path most taken. These people also have serious questions about their affiliative faith. They, too, lack the courage to risk relationships or reputation or rejection by honestly pursuing their questions. They don't want to clash with friends, family, or tradition. Even so, they are well aware that suppressed anger is toxic. They know that stuffed feelings can show up in some terribly destructive ways: clinical depression, sexual acting out, or substance abuse, to name a few. So they stay put—but learn to unplug the force of their questions.

They refine the art of tuning out their own consciences. They simply capitulate at "affiliative" levels—they "go along to get along"; they stop growing, go spiritually numb, and play out the mundane church game. This option is, of course, the most dangerous of all. They no longer seek an ever-deepening "relationship" with God. All the "verb" has been drained from their faith, leaving at best the dry and shriveled "noun" called "religion."

Note: One clear difference between mere religion and authentic relationship with God is precisely the difference between levels 2 and 4, between "affiliative" faith and "owned" faith. That is, a person may hold to "the full biblical truth" on doctrine (if any of us knows what all that means) and still be merely *religious*, if his or her views have their source in "affiliation" and not in an honest hunger for an ever-deepening relationship with God. Another person, on the other hand, might have some unbiblical and ill-developed theology and still enjoy an authentic *relationship* with God, if indeed he or she "owns" that faith—that is, if he or she hungrily pursues God with integrity, at all costs.

The person who chooses this third option can eventually *dismantle the very capacity to believe.* Although these persons conform—and maybe even stay in some congregational "leadership role"—something about them will no longer ring true and they will inadvertently become a drag on the faith and character development of people around them. They will not really have the interests of the flock at heart. Having lost character at the center of their souls, they will become vulnerable to all sorts of sin and deception, as well as to power plays and manipulation. And the more intimately their "sheep" get to know them, the less they respect them and trust them.

Fyodor Dostoevsky paints a dark picture of where a closed, defensive kind of mind-set that lacks integrity can ultimately lead us:

> When we lie to ourselves, and believe our own lies, we become unable to recognize truth, either in ourselves or in anyone else, and we end up losing respect for ourselves and for others. When we have no respect for anyone, we can no longer love, and in order to divert ourselves, having no love in us, we yield to our impulses, indulge in the lowest forms of pleasure, and behave in the end like an animal, in satisfying our vices. And it all comes from lying—lying to others and to ourselves.[6]

Of course, not every person who stalls at affiliative faith will wind up in such an extreme spiritually bankrupt state. Social pressure and fear of being found out will often keep him or her within some boundaries. But God cares about our hearts—and at the end of the day, it is the heart that inevitably shows through to God-hungry people.

section two: A HEART OF INTEGRITY

If you aspire to be a spiritual leader, a shepherd of God's people, then remember what matters most: your character. Ask yourself, "From the core of my heart, am I a person of integrity? Am I genuinely seeking to be 'the kind of person that God-hungry people want to be like'?" If you answer with a painfully honest no, then whatever you do, don't let anyone call you his or her shepherd!

On the other hand, however, God-hungry people will trust and follow a shepherd with genuine integrity of character. This kind of shepherd owns his or her faith, yet expresses interest in your "searching" questions, knowing that this kind of "searching" gently leads the lambs toward mature, "owned" faith. *That* is the kind of person God-hungry people want to be like!

CARDIOVASCULAR WORKOUTS
FOR SHEPHERD HEARTS

How we function in "a system" is shaped, first of all, by how we function in a "family system." To begin examining these "roots of integrity," take a pencil and pad, and write down your reflections on the following questions.

1. How would you relate your sense of call into ministry to your nuclear or extended family?

2. What is your place in the constellation of your family of origin: oldest, youngest, middle? Were you a brother with younger sisters? Younger brothers? Older sisters? Older brothers? How did the unique spot in the family that you occupied help shape you in learning to relate to the same sex and to the opposite sex?

3. How would you draw your own family diagram? Try to go back at least two generations (to your grandparents). Talk to people in the family to gather as many details and stories as possible. What do you really know about these people? Where has there been conflict? Where have symptoms occurred? Become as curious about this family as you can. Ask lots of questions. Make them your own personal research project.

4. If you were to make it a goal to establish a personal, one-to-one relationship with every living member of this family, where would you start? Why? Which ones would be the most difficult to engage?

5. If either of your parents is deceased, how would you go about re-engaging that relationship? Where could you go to find the

information about the dead parent that you would need if you were to understand him or her more fully as a person?

6. As you think about this family, where do you find yourself most tempted to place blame?

7. If you attempted to engage your family in an effort to differentiate, what issues would arise? How would you think about going among them and being different than you usually are? How would they likely react? How would you think about responding to the reaction differently? In which relationship would change be most difficult to sustain?[7]

six

PATHWAY OF INTEGRITY

No happiness without virtue; no virtue without wisdom;
no wisdom with love.

—Author Unknown

The mercury had dipped to thirty-two degrees below zero that cold Canadian day in 1936, when hardy homesteaders lugged a cattle trough into my homesteading parents' kitchen. They hauled water from the well, heated it on our coal-fed stove, and then filled the trough deeply enough to baptize Mom and Dad, who had made firm personal commitments to trust Jesus as their Savior and Lord and to follow him no matter where he took them, regardless of the cost. After my parents made this choice, their social circles excluded them for a time, because they dared to value and embrace authentic relationship with God through their "owned" faith even more than the security of their circle of friends.

I am proud of this heritage.

I have always admired the courage of my parents and the honest frontier environment that nurtured their freedom. But in moments of introspection, I feel puzzled by my own attitudes: Why do I admire my parents' courage, yet get "antsy" when my children, in their hunger for God—and in the spirit of their grandparents—sometimes "own" viewpoints that don't match mine? Would I discourage my children from developing integrity and God-hunger, merely to have them agree with me? Would I want them to "stake homesteads" and become "permanent settlers" on the theological territory my pilgrim parents saw only as a "frontier" of grace?

DON'T SHRINK BACK

Of course, I cherish my understanding of the faith deeply enough that I want my children to share it. Yet, I pray that they will love God enough to pursue his truth *as they understand it* even if their search leads them along pathways different from my own, and even if it leads both them and me through great pain.

The fact is, pursuing truth will at times crush and break all of us. But, I implore you, my shepherding friends, let us not shrink back from this pain!

Merle Crowell tells a story about a Greenland Eskimo who joined an arctic expedition back in the 1920s. For his faithful guide service, his employers rewarded him with a visit to New York City. Dazzled by the wonders, he couldn't wait to tell his friends back home in Greenland. Once home, he described "stacks of igloos reaching into the clouds" and "crowded igloos moving along the trail."

The simple village people found his report too disturbing to believe. So they listened with fish-eyed stares, tagged him "Sagdluk" (that is, "The Liar"), and shunned him. By the time of his death, his original name had long been forgotten; he carried the name "Liar" to his grave.

Later, Knud Rasmussen made a trip to the frozen North, guided by another Greenland Eskimo named Mitek. Mitek, too, got a trip to New York and he, too, felt dazzled by the city. But remembering the fate of Sagdluk, he cooked up stories that his Eskimo friends could swallow. He and Rasmussen had merely "paddled a big kayak on a wide river called Hudson," he said. And they saw "lots of ducks, and geese—and some seals." His friends felt comfortable with this account. Thus, Mitek—the real liar—actually gained a place of extraordinary respect among his home villagers, while the man who had told the truth was called "Liar" and died in ignominy.

FACE THE CHILL WIND

This should not surprise us. Those hardy souls who with integrity pursue truth at all costs often face such a chill wind. As my dear friend Ann Silkman says, "People who dance to a different beat have always been called insane by those who can't hear the music."

Remember Jeremiah the prophet, who told his people the troubling truth—and was thrown in a well as a result? And Stephen testified that he saw Jesus—so his peers stoned him to death. Luther risked his life by telling the unpopular truth at the Council of Worms. Most especially, remember Jesus on the cross, who in the darkness cried out loud, "My God, my God, why have you forsaken me?"[1]

Surely we cannot expect to be given freedom of conscience through some church policy! Nor by popular vote. Nor can the government legislate character. Oh, no. Genuine character is in the *heart*.

Stephen Crane, author of the famous early twentieth-century novel *The Red Badge of Courage*, confronted the pain of integrity in his poem "The Wayfarer":

> *The wayfarer,*
>
> *Perceiving the pathway to truth*
>
> *Was struck with astonishment.*
>
> *It was thickly grown with weeds.*
>
> *"Ha," he said,*
>
> *"I see that none has passed here*
>
> *In a long time."*

section two: A HEART OF INTEGRITY

Later he saw that each weed

Was a singular knife.

"Well," he mumbled at last,

"Doubtless there are other roads."[2]

Perhaps Stephen Crane was describing himself. Not long after he wrote this poem, and at a very young age, he took his own life. Or perhaps he is telling the story of all who fear the sharp, intruding edges that cut away faith's childhood and goad us toward "owned" faith and beyond.

Without doubt, following the path of true character and integrity can mean painful choices for the spiritual leader. There is no denying that. But nonetheless, real integrity is essential to authentic, spiritual shepherding, especially in our postmodern environment, where people value authenticity and experience far more than credentials and rational proof. If they get even a whiff of the notion that a leader is more concerned about his reputation than the truth of God, it is "game over." That would-be leader will have no credibility with those he seeks to lead.

Oswald Sanders challenges us,

No one need aspire to leadership in the work of God who is not prepared to pay a price greater than his contemporaries and colleagues are ready to pay. True leadership always exacts a heavy toll on the whole man, and the more effective the leadership is, the higher the price to be paid.[3]

To persons of character, the approving smile of Jesus means infinitely more than keeping their jobs or receiving accolades from their fellows. Rather, they seem strangely hungry for "the praise that comes from the only God." In fact, without this raw integrity we would-be Christian leaders may not even be real believers! At least, in the "verb" sense.

Remember, it was Jesus who said, "*How can you believe* if you accept praise from one another, yet make no effort to obtain the praise that comes from the only God?"[4]

WHEN NO ONE SEES

For three thousand years, spiritual leaders have prayed for integrity of heart. That renowned early human shepherd of God's people, King David, was chosen for his integrity, which he learned from working among literal sheep. "From [shepherding] the sheep [God] brought [David] to be the shepherd of his people. . . . And David shepherded them with integrity of heart."[5]

Out there in that lonely pasture, when dangers threatened his father's sheep, David might just as easily have fled; his father would have been none the wiser. But he stayed and fought the lions and bears, even though no one was watching! Integrity, after all, is measured by what one does in private, when no one else will know. In the absolute anonymity of the sheep pasture, when no one saw and no one knew, David repeatedly risked his life for a few stinking, stubborn sheep that could give him no personal rewards.

But God was David's audience, and David's own heart was his supervisor. This great shepherd of God's people prayed fervently for a heart wide open to God's searching eye: "You desire truth in the inner parts; you teach me wisdom in the inmost place."[6] And David tells us that God will use a man "in whose spirit is no deceit."[7]

We live in a cynical world. Even kids are wise to the duplicity of

> Real integrity is essential to authentic, spiritual shepherding, especially in our postmodern environment, where people value authenticity and experience far more than credentials and rational proof.

some government leaders, televangelists, and hucksters of Madison Avenue. Most folks desperately need to know a few good people who are honest to the core. Families need them. Schools need them, too, as well as governments. And above all, the flock of God desperately needs shepherds who always shoot straight. At heart, a shepherd of God's flock must—absolutely *must*—be a person of integrity.

DAMAGING LAPSE OR WINDOW TO CHARACTER?

Of what value to a God-hungry person is a "Christian leader" with little integrity? I think of the story of a stressed-out Christian woman's conference speaker who was impatiently tailgating a man's car at rush hour on a busy boulevard. Suddenly the light in front of the man turned yellow. Even though he probably could have beaten the red light, he did the honest thing and stopped at the crosswalk.

This infuriated the "Christian" speaker. She hit the horn, screaming in frustration at her missed chance to get through the intersection. Then, in mid-rant, she heard a tap on her window and looked up into the very serious face of a police officer. He ordered her out, handcuffed her, and took her to the station where she was searched, fingerprinted, photographed, and locked in a cell.

After some time the cell opened and an officer escorted her back to the booking desk, where the arresting officer waited with her personal effects.

"I'm very sorry for this mistake," the arresting officer explained. "You see, I pulled up behind your car while you were blowing your horn, flipping the guy off in front of you, and cursing a blue streak. When I noticed the Choose Life license-plate holder, the What Would Jesus Do? and Follow Me to Sunday School bumper stickers, plus the chrome-plated fish emblem on the trunk, I just *knew* this had to be a stolen car."

NO MATTER THE COST

The authentic shepherd lives his or her life with integrity and is guided by principles, not politics. He or she does not feel threatened by group pressure or intimidated by public opinion.

That shepherd feels far more concerned about the needs of the flock and what will benefit them spiritually than about avoiding criticism. He or she will never, ever knowingly hurt an individual to elevate self with the group. And the shepherd of courage will unflinchingly seek the glory of God and do the will of God as he or she understands it, no matter what comes.

Bottom line, a person of integrity has the courage to seek God's will and to love and serve God's people—no matter what it costs him or her personally—*even when no one is looking.*

CARDIOVASCULAR WORKOUTS
FOR SHEPHERD HEARTS

One Christian leader expressed regret in retirement years: "If only I had been as good as the people thought I was." How do we minimize the likelihood of winding up our careers with similar regrets?

Find two hours and a quiet place to thoughtfully work through the following questions, adapted from a list by H. B. London and Neil Wiseman.[8] Journal your reflections as you go.

1. How squeaky clean is my handling of church money?

2. How ethically authentic is my use of time?

3. How much disparity is there between my beliefs and the quality of my teaching and the shepherding care I provide?

4. How enjoyable and fulfilling is my marriage, in light of what God intended?

5. How many of the people I lead believe me to be unequivocally trustworthy?

6. How often do I deceive myself with chronic self-deceptions?

7. How much do my wife (husband) and children have to compete with my ministry?

8. In what ways do I accept my part in failures in my life and church?

9. How close have I come to flirting with potentially destructive relationships?

10. How likely might I be to tell half-truths and exaggerate my successes?

11. How consistent is my ministry with what I really believe God wants my life to be?

seven

A HEART SHAPED BY THE HOLINESS OF GOD

I am the LORD your God; consecrate yourselves
and be holy, because I am holy.

—Leviticus 11:44

H. G. Wells told the story of a fictitious New England bishop revered for his sensitivity and wisdom. People freely told him their troubles, and he would usually ask, "Have you prayed about it?" He had discovered that if he spoke that question in just the right tone, it seemed to settle things a bit.

The bishop himself, however, never prayed much. He felt no need of prayer. He had things all wrapped up in a tight package—until one day his life tumbled in. He found himself so overwhelmed that he decided to take his own advice and pray.

On Saturday evening he entered the cathedral, stumbled down to the front, fell on his knees, knelt on the crimson carpet, and folded his hands before the altar. He could not help but think how childlike he had become. Then he began to pray, "Oh God . . ."

Suddenly a voice, crisp and business-like, boomed out from somewhere above him.

"Well, what is it?"

Next day, as the story goes, worshipers who came to the Sunday service found the bishop lying facedown on the floor. When they turned him over, they discovered he was stone dead, with lines of horror still etched upon his face.

A lot of us who talk a great deal about God would be scared to death if we saw Him face-to-face. Yet that is where God calls his shepherds and spiritual leaders to live, face-to-face with him in all his terrifying holiness. To see God is to see myself more clearly; that is the central key to becoming "the kind of person God-hungry people want to be like."

God is totally powerful and completely in-the-know. His justice is total. His truth is exhaustive. His love is infinite. He is holy! Set apart, different from all others. R. C. Sproul describes holiness this way:

When the Bible calls God holy, it means primarily that God is transcendentally separate. To be holy is to be "other," to be different in a special way. Look carefully at the following list of things the Bible speaks of as holy:

holy ground	holy ones
holy Sabbath	holy city
holy nation	holy linen coat
holy house	holy tithe
holy anointing oil	holy field
holy convocation	

This list is by no means exhaustive. The things that are holy are things that are set apart, separated from the rest. They have been consecrated, separated from the commonplace, unto the Lord and to his service.

Where does purity come in? When things are made holy, when they are consecrated, they are set apart unto purity. They are to be used in a pure way. They are to reflect purity as well as simple apartness. But the point we must remember is that the idea of the holy is never exhausted by the idea of purity. It includes purity but is much more than that. It is purity and transcendence. It is a transcendent purity.[1]

Indeed, there is far more to holiness than sexual purity! Without question, however, a person shaped by God's holiness is ethically and morally pure. It is this particular expression of holiness that we pursue in the following pages.

HIDDEN SIN

Holiness and hidden sin cannot coexist. Burton Coffman, a veteran minister (who turned 100 this year!), pointed out something to me in a very earthy way nearly three decades ago. He heard me teach that the taproot of faith is a decision of the will. After the sermon Burton beelined to me and boomed, "Decision of the will. That's right, boy. But it's also a moral decision."

I asked him to help me understand what he meant.

"Well," he explained, "we have a way of adjusting our theology to fit our morality. For example, you show me a Christian leader who is getting too sophisticated and broad-minded for the gospel, and I'll show you a Christian leader who may be shacked up with his secretary!"

Burton understood how hidden sin, not dealt with, devastates the convictions and thus the usefulness of a Christian leader, even when no one knows what happened. Of course, all varieties of hidden sin have the same effect, not just the scarlet sin in Coffman's colorful quote. Sin not dealt with, big or small, is a silent killer of spiritual leadership. Why? Because it saps the winsomeness from a shepherd's heart. What is more, it is an affront to God's holiness!

A ONE-PERSON PERSON

When sketching out the heart of elders, Paul the apostle includes the "husband of but one wife" as one ingredient.[2] On the surface this seems to address polygamy, common at the time. But multiple wives likely wasn't the problem in Ephesus; fidelity in marriage definitely was. A better translation aims the verse at the heart of the shepherd: a "one-woman man." That points to an entirely different issue.

A lot of first-century men proudly strove to be a three-woman man. First, there was a slave girl whose responsibilities went beyond chores and household duties; she provided sexual favors for the man of the house. The second woman was often the temple prostitute, intended for sexual gratification as acts of worship, of all things. And third was the wife, used largely for breeding and for keeping track of the kids.

So calling every spiritual shepherd to be a "one-woman man" was radical. It had nothing to do with marital history and everything to do with character. As my friend Brad Tuggle says, "Even today, a married man could be a two- or three-woman man, if not physically, at least in his heart. Jesus said lust is mental adultery. When you reach the point of 'I would if I could,' you have already crossed the line. Even pursuing illicit sexual relationships in your mind is a violation of sexual purity and does not honor your wife. Adultery begins in the heart before it happens in the bedroom."[3]

And as Paul the apostle explains, "We take captive every thought to make it obedient to Christ."[4]

Sexual purity is only one reflection of holiness, but sexual purity provides one of the surest tests of character. Shepherds of God's church must be "one-woman men," faithful in every way to their wives, especially in our day of the anonymous Internet and sexual permissiveness. Of course, the call to sexual purity applies to women as well. It is every bit as important that a Christian woman who "spiritually shepherds" anyone also live as a "one-man woman." God calls every one of us to this standard—not just shepherds and not just men, but all men and women who follow Christ. Those in leadership roles must take special care to safeguard their moral and sexual purity.

FALLOUT FROM TAKING THE BIG HIT

King David discovered the importance of this principle in spades. David may have written Psalm 32 soon after the prophet Nathan confronted him about David's devastating twin sins—adultery and murder. For a long while David had hidden his sin and struggled with his duplicity. But by the time he penned Psalm 32, possibly David had repeatedly stared into the midnight darkness, imagining the face of Uriah, whom David had so cruelly betrayed. And surely David had locked eyes with a brokenhearted, but offended, Holy God.

> When I kept silent, my bones wasted away
> > through my groaning all day long.
> For day and night your hand was heavy upon me;
> > my strength was sapped as in the heat of summer.[5]

David's guilt also apparently produced psychosomatic illness:

Because of your wrath there is no health in my body. . . .
> My back is filled with searing pain . . .
> > my strength fails me; even the light has gone from my eyes.[6]

It would appear that David's duplicity even led him into social shallows: "My friends and companions avoid me because of my wounds; my neighbors stay far away."[7] But, David—is it really they who stay away from you, or you who avoid them?

Years ago and far away, a coworker with whom I had felt very close subtly began moving toward more impersonal conversation and slowly distanced himself from me. I searched my soul, wondering if I had offended him. Then he began avoiding staff-group devotions, even subtly making light of the need our team felt for such times. He explained that he was wired differently and that he did not get his spiritual batteries charged through "that emotional sort of thing." He even implied that some of us were imposing our needs on the rest of the group. Self-doubt wobbled me. Time revealed, however, that this brother had drifted into the grip of gross immorality. Of course he did not want to remain close to his fellow shepherds and be open with them—much less approach the gaze of the Holy One.

We're no different. In such a state, you or I will likely be either unwilling or afraid to be known by God or anyone else. This will drive us to spiritual and social shallows—and will keep us from "smelling like sheep."

Believe me, I know! I, too, have cycled through spells when the veneer looked thick and glossy on the outside, but in my heart I kept God at a distance. I have traveled through tunnels of darkness, outwardly gregarious, but intimate and open with no one. Have you? The name of our sin is irrelevant.

> Be self-controlled and alert. Your enemy the devil
> prowls around like a roaring lion looking for someone
> to devour. Resist him, standing firm in the faith . . .[8]

Every person who allows people to call him or her "my shepherd" must ask himself or herself, *Am I willing to deal with sin that is distancing me from people, separating me from God, and resulting in stale and impotent pseudo-ministry—where God-hungry people could find little in me that they would want for themselves?* Hidden sin will always blunt our usefulness to God, even if no one ever knows! If you are unwilling to confess and address hidden sin, by all means, step out of your role as a "Christian leader."

HEALING AGAIN

Only one path leads back to courage: confession and repentance. Listen again to King David, our ancient fellow struggler:

> Then I acknowledged my sin to you and did not cover up my iniquity.
> I said, "I will confess my transgressions to the LORD"
> —and you forgave the guilt of my sin.[9]

An open, penitent, confessing, and obedient life is indispensable to the heart of a shepherd. Centuries ago Thomas à Kempis warned, "At the day of judgment we shall not be asked what we have read, but what we have done; not how eloquently we have spoken, but how holy we have lived."[10]

Wonderful release and renewal are available through genuine repentance, confession, and forgiveness. "Therefore let everyone who is godly pray to you while you may be found; surely when the mighty waters rise, they will not reach him."[11] Walking the road toward holiness with him will help you regain lost courage and restore faded vibrancy. God has promised his presence and power for the journey! Now is the time to reach out and claim it.

CARDIOVASCULAR WORKOUTS
FOR SHEPHERD HEARTS

In the early days of Methodism, John Wesley called lay leaders to a higher code. He established converts through a group atmosphere of active faith and personal accountability. Get with another trusted shepherd on a regular basis and ask each other Wesley's questions:[12]

1. What known sins have you committed since our last meeting?

2. What temptations have assaulted you?

3. How were you delivered?

4. What have you thought, said, or done, about which you doubt whether it be sin or not?

5. Do you have anything you desire to keep secret?

eight

A PATH
TO PURITY

Purity of heart is to will one thing.

—Søren Kierkegaard

A friend in the Southeast knew a Christian leader who, although a good man, allowed his insecurities to make it very difficult for him to be honest about his own frailties. One Sunday he stood before his church and, in a moment of false bravado, asserted that "no woman can tempt me!" A certain little lady sitting in the congregation swiveled her high-heeled shoe back and forth on her toe, thinking, Well, we'll just see about this!

Before many weeks had passed, that man toppled from his perch, devastating both his life and his usefulness as a shepherd. The fault did not lay with the man's ideals. But his denial of his own vulnerabilities ended up ambushing him.

If this poor man had openly acknowledged his vulnerability to a trusted confidant, he might have averted his folly. And it would have been a decisive and wise step up the pathway of holiness. "He that has ears to hear, let him hear."

TRANSPARENCY

A first step toward staying straight is transparency. Transparency means openness and honesty about ourselves and living in a confessional posture. We need transparency to effectively deal with every aspect of our vulnerability to any sin, not just lust.

My own ineptitude in so many areas of life forces me to live in a confessional and grace-dependent posture. You are as capable of rottenness as I am; Scripture says so. So was the apostle Paul, and he never forgot it for a minute. His claim to be "chief of sinners"[1] was neither hyperbole nor false modesty. His humble-sounding confession was no mere ploy to leap the intimidation barrier so he could identify with us "lesser mortals." Rather, it described Paul's personal reality. Make sure you don't miss his verb tense: not "was" but "am" chief of sinners. Present tense!

We don't know the apostle's biggest areas of vulnerability, but we do know that his transparency led him to walk life's pathway in a confessional posture. Today's shepherds need to walk the same way.

Don't imagine, however, that I am suggesting you neurotically dump your guts at every conversation. We must be discriminating as well as sensitive to others. We dare not be totally transparent with any and everybody. We had best choose carefully to whom we open our lives, and where. Still, the Bible calls us to transparency: to awareness of our vulnerability, to honesty with trusted confidants, and to dependency on our God and his grace. James wrote, "Confess your sins to each other and pray for each other so that you may be healed."[2]

> The Bible calls us to transparency: to awareness of our vulnerability, to honesty with trusted confidants, and to dependency on our God and his grace.

Neither am I suggesting mere self "down-talk." Self-bashing undercuts credibility, too. Such prattle often merely parades a false humility. I do not need to perennially bad-mouth one of God's sanctified ones, even if that person happens to be myself. Nevertheless, the moment I do anything in order to appear better or stronger than I really am—no matter how small it may seem—I have begun a deadly deception and set myself up for bigger and more horrendous things to come.

This means that, in some situations, public transparency may be helpful. I know of one minister who drove up to the church at midnight to drop in and encourage the music and drama groups practicing for a Christmas program. Since he arrived late and the lot appeared empty, he wheeled into the fire lane, jumped out of the car, and ran in. No big deal. After all, it was just for a moment, and he was the minister! The next day, one of his staff members informed him that a teenager spotted the car and had wondered out loud, "What jerk would block the fire lane outside a room full of people?"

The following Sunday that minister told the whole church about the incident and apologized for his presumption and recklessness. He even asked the church to keep holding him accountable: "Stay in my face. I need you, or I could be a wreck looking for a place to happen." This shepherd rightly understood that ignoring one fairly innocent act could easily become the first self-deluding step in a direction that could ultimately end in disaster. His open confession before the church kept him aware of his own vulnerability. Paradoxically, his openness also increased his credibility with his people.

ACCOUNTABILITY

Along with the need for transparency, I am discovering the value of accountability. Warning: while my being accountable to you is of absolutely no spiritual value to either one of us if you demand it of me, it is of inestimable value if I request it of you. This kind of accountability must include accountability to both the flock we lead and our fellow shepherds.

Some years back in a state distant from my home, I spoke on the need for accountability. Later a young man cornered me privately with an unusual request. He described himself as a "flasher." He had periodically flashed for a number of years, but so far he had not been caught. He convinced me that he genuinely wanted to stop his destructive and God-dishonoring behavior. He had tried every remedy, but nothing had worked. Then he made this strange request: "You have convinced me that I might be helped by making myself accountable to someone. Would you let me be accountable to you?"

I protested, "But I live in another part of the country, and I will rarely see you. Besides, I scarcely know you. Wouldn't it be better for you to be accountable to someone here?" But I could not persuade him to muster the courage to confess to someone in his home church. So I reluctantly agreed to exchange periodic phone calls with him, but didn't really expect much from such a flimsy agreement.

The phone calls continued occasionally for some two years. From the very first one, he told me that he had stopped flashing. I saw him again several years later, and he said he had lost even the compulsion to flash.

Something powerful resides in the anticipation of frank and loving questions. Of course, professional counselors use such contracts routinely as a therapeutic technique to treat problems ranging all across the emotional landscape.

A GIFT FROM A FRIEND

I know of a number of Christian leaders who refuse to travel unless accompanied by a family member or a Christian brother, again to practice and model accountability. I know why. I often find myself on the road . . . far from home . . . where no one knows me. Maybe I get to my hotel exhausted, maybe even hurt or depressed. And then I walk into a strange room—all alone. Sometimes evil seems to lurk everywhere. And without accountability, in a weary and depressed and lonely state, I feel vulnerable.

Probably you understand. You, too, have stood at such dark, anonymous doorways. "Often," you say. So you know what I mean!

Let me pass you a bright secret for such dark places. Years back, a friend gave me a strong weapon for times like those. He taught me to step through the door, set down my luggage, fire up my laptop, and open a file in "My Documents" under "Prayer of Cleansing." Then I pray the prayer aloud. It goes like this:

Lord, I claim this place for your purposes. I stand on the truth of your Word: "The scepter of the wicked will not remain over the land allotted to the righteous" (Psalm 125:3). I believe you have given me this place for today. I dedicate it to you and ask you to fill it with your holy presence. I separate myself from any iniquity that has occurred here in past times. I apply the power of Jesus's blood to remove any desecration of God's name in this place. I ask you, in Jesus's authority, to set watching angels around this property, protecting your servant from the work of the evil one.

If this is a hotel or motel room, I will add the following:

Father, I ask for your holy presence and holy angels to linger here, to touch the lives of those who inhabit the room after me. Bring conviction to their hearts and draw them to seek after you.

I stand on the authority of the Lord Jesus Christ, whose name is above every name, to weaken the power of evil in this place. Through the blood of Christ, I remove all desecration of the name of God that was prompted, whether by human or demonic beings. I command all enemies of Jesus Christ that have access to this place, or who may be here now . . . to leave. Go now where you are ordered to go, by the voice of the Holy Spirit. I claim this property for the Kingdom of Light. I order all darkness to flee, in the name of Jesus the King.[3]

After entering the room, you must pray this prayer first, before anything else. ANYTHING else! Sometimes I sit on the edge of the bed and pray, until a sense of security descends. When I pray the prayer aloud, firmly, and resolutely—from the heart—I begin to feel much safer and my room seems cleaner and healthier. The dark corners, once seemingly inhabited by sinister forces, seem to fill with loving-kindness.

It also helps to remember that God left us at least three powerful promises:

1. "I am with you always, to the very end of the age."[4]

2. "He will not let you be tempted beyond what you can bear. But . . . he will also provide a way out so that you can stand up under it."[5]

3. "Your Father in heaven [will] give good gifts to those who ask him!"[6]

And God has kept his promises! My friend gave me a great gift in this prayer; that's why I am eager to pass it along. So together we can be reminded of the infinitely more precious gift of God's presence.

PRE-ARRANGED ACCOUNTABILITY

When I travel without Carolyn or some other Christian brother or family member, I plan ahead to "check in" with Christian friends as soon as I hit the permissive disconnectedness of whatever distant city. I have done this for decades. I inform Carolyn where she can reach me any time, day or night. I want my life to be accountable to those I love and trust because I don't trust myself.

You shouldn't trust yourself, either! Church leaders who do not make themselves accountable place themselves in grave danger. At the very least, they leave themselves open to false rumors.

"Neurotically scrupulous," did I hear you say? Maybe. But I don't think so. We are not to measure our spiritual maturity by the willpower we can muster while exposed to our strongest temptation. Quite the contrary! We demonstrate our spiritual maturity best when, fully aware of our most dangerous vulnerabilities, we carefully preplan our defense. We are wise when we make ourselves accountable to trusted fellow Christians who know us well enough to spot danger signals and who love us enough to look us in the eye and say so.

In his book *How to Swim with the Sharks without Getting Eaten Alive*, Harvey Mackay reveals a unique clue to the ongoing influence of Billy Graham. Other television evangelists have come and gone, but Billy Graham continues to draw respect and large TV audiences. Mackay gives a two-word explanation for Graham's staying power: Grady Wilson.

Billy Graham made it a point to make himself accountable to his longtime friend. Mackay credits Grady Wilson with steering Billy Graham away from several potential disasters that would have damaged his ministry. Graham has long and humbly heeded the advice of his employee and friend.

Blessed is the shepherd who is willing to make himself accountable! Every shepherd needs a Grady Wilson.

REFLECTION

Besides transparency and accountability to others, I also need reflection on my own heart. My journal helps me a great deal here. Writing down my reflections tends to make them specific and clear and moves me past "stuck" places.

By journaling I can also periodically review and gain perspective on the trends of my life. Sometimes I feel real surprise at the progress I have made. At other times I am struck at how long and how frequently I have been mired in the same sin or how deeply some resentment has invaded my personality. David prayed, "Who can discern his [own] errors?"[7] This kind of inventory helps me more quickly spot the hidden sins that threaten my usefulness as a shepherd.

But another word of caution here. We can easily slip into compulsive spiritual navel-gazing, which often winds up being a most insidious mutation of self-centeredness. For this reason, let me point to the crucial place of praise in our reflective times.

Praise focuses us beyond ourselves. I have a growing appreciation of the power of pure, personal praise. Consequently, I make it a habit to both begin and end my prayer and reflection time with praise.

PRAISE

Praise may take many forms. Usually my own praise is internal and silent, but often it is aloud and occasionally (dare I admit it?) with hands raised, shouting at the top of my lungs. Sometimes I repeat a psalm. Sometimes I simply reflect on the goodness of God and let "stream of consciousness" roll. More often, however, some structured resources help.

We see a variety of praise expressions among God's people in the Bible. Some shouted and sang and clapped and raised their hands—and even danced! Some wrote poetry. Some sat in silence. But one way or another, the Word of God is full of praise.

Praise makes glad the heart of God, of course. Praise refines our spirits. It drives away despair. But it also changes us! The psalmist said, "You turned my wailing into dancing."[8] It refines the conscience, strengthens faith, and sensitizes the soul to the presence and majesty of God. And it is almost impossible to keep looking regularly into the face of the Holy One, praising him with our full beings, and at the same time persist in our little rebellions.

Praise gives strength for the journey. It emboldens our hearts. Praise is a powerful pathway to purity. What shepherd can come away from genuine praise without his or her heart being changed? In consistent praise our hearts are pressed against the glory of God. And as John Piper says, "The glory of God weans us from the breast of the world."[9]

In summary: seek a heart of holiness. Let us, fellow travelers, keep taking wise and decisive steps on the upward pathway: transparency, accountability, reflection, and praise. These mold us toward holiness; they shape within us "the heart of a shepherd."

CARDIOVASCULAR WORKOUTS
FOR SHEPHERD HEARTS

Use or adapt the following accountability questions, developed by Charles Swindoll, with yourself, with staff, or in other settings where appropriate:

1. Have you been with a woman (a man) anywhere this past week that might be seen as compromising?

2. Have any of your financial dealings lacked integrity?

3. Have you exposed yourself to any sexually explicit material?

4. Have you spent adequate time in Bible study and prayer?

5. Have you given priority time to your family?

6. Have you fulfilled the mandates of your calling?

7. Have you just lied to me?[10]

A HEART
FOR PEOPLE

Wisdom is knowing what to do next; virtue is doing it.

—David Starr Jordan

nine

IT'S ALL ABOUT PEOPLE

So God created man in his own image . . .
—Genesis 1:27

Carolyn and I sat aboard an aircraft in Victoria, British Columbia, ready for departure. From our little oval window we spotted several luggage wagons parked on the tarmac, all piled high with magazines. Then we noticed that each one of those hundreds of magazines bore the same name: *People*. All over the continent, millions of people would soon slap down five dollars a throw just to read about the goings-on of people they didn't even know! Amazing, considering that most of us get our fill of people every day.

It set us to thinking: the only real difference between *People* magazine and most other magazines sold today is the name! Most magazines are about people. *Life* magazine is about people. *Sports Illustrated* is about people. *Time*, *Newsweek*, even the *Wall Street Journal* are all about people. This shouts something about human nature. We people are all enormously fascinated with each other.

We sing primarily about people. TV mostly pictures people. At the movies we pay good money to sit in the dark and watch shadow pictures of imaginary people. We read novels to get inside the psyches of people. Sometimes, for recreation, we go to the mall to watch people. Even in daily conversation we mostly discuss people. We are driven by our passion for people. In fact, our fascination with people reveals how we are created in the image of God, for people are the bull's-eye on the Chief Shepherd's target.

WHEN WE MISS THE TARGET

Since we people are so intrinsically interested in people, if we focus on anything else (ideas, tasks, status, or institutions), we do serious damage to the central matrix of our own humanity—beyond the damage we do to the people we claim to be shepherding.

A co-worker drove this home to me in a very personal way a few years back. She had been in our office for only a few weeks, but something wasn't going right. So I sat down to chat with her, hoping to work through *her* problem.

"Something seems to be bothering you," I said. "Can I help?" I wasn't quite prepared for what I heard next.

"You are plastic!" she said for openers. "You want this church to be user-friendly, but *you* aren't. You are inaccessible and insensitive. You constantly break appointments because you're 'too busy' with what *you* want to do. And you are making the people in this office feel like peons. You are supposed to be a spiritual leader, but I see you as completely unapproachable."

I felt stunned. *Me?* Unapproachable? Insensitive? Surely not *me*! I tried to deny her accusations, rationalize them, and blame everybody else. But . . . really, she was dead right. There was nothing to do but face my insensitivity, own it, and apologize to her . . . and one by one, to the whole team. And then I began the task of getting back on track.

Yet how had this happened? Didn't I have a reputation for being warm, approachable, and people oriented? Hadn't I built a long and visible track record of good relationships?

This painful moment of truth forced me to look honestly at the past many months. Everything seemed a blur. My pocket calendar looked as cluttered as a city dump: far too many speaking engagements, way too much travel, two new books, a new church, helping launch a new journal, teaching a graduate course. And page after page of appointments moved or canceled. The pace had gradually accelerated, reaching an all-time high over the previous few weeks (as I fought a contract deadline, ironically, on a book about *relationships!*). And as my internal engines exceeded the redline, I had become less and less available, more and more self-absorbed.

Me? Unapproachable? Insensitive? Surely not *me*!

I *am* a people person, but I had allowed myself to become task-driven. For months I had not only been neglecting people, but leaving hurt and disillusioned bodies in my wake, jeopardizing the very things I really believe are most important. As I got less sensitive to people, I drifted ever closer toward disaster.

And need I say it? I certainly was *not* the kind of person God-hungry people want to be like.

Somehow I doubt I am the only person to wrestle with this issue. Long experience tells me that most, if not all, shepherds—even the most people-oriented—can easily drift toward tasks and away from people.

God's number one priority is *people.* To do his main thing, God became "a people and moved to live among people." The Chief Shepherd "pitched his tent in our pasture." Jesus was "God in a body," out there on the people turf. For Jesus, people are "Job One." That means for all authentic followers of Jesus, especially the shepherds of God's flock, people must become top priority, as well.

God, who is in "the people business," has also called us into people-centered living. Thus, the most God-like thing a shepherd can do is to give people the priority God gives us and to treat people the way Jesus did.

RELATIONSHIPS: THE SHEPHERD'S WORKPLACE

When the crowds asked Jesus, "What is the greatest commandment?" He answered, "Love the Lord your God with all your heart and with all your soul and with all your mind and with all your strength."[2] That raised no eyebrows and rocked no boats. It was merely the familiar ancient *Shema*, which bookended all synagogue meetings.

But then Jesus unexpectedly added a line: "Love your neighbor as yourself."[3] Oops! Now, wait a minute, Jesus! Everything was fine like it was. "Love God" has a nice ring to it. Sounds religious—and it can be kept comfortably abstract.

But that added line slammed the abstract down onto the concrete.

The way Jesus put it, we express our love for God, not in pews, pulpits, stained-glass tones, or doctrinal hair-splitting, but in relationships among people—in the way you and I get along with him and her and them. If being with God on Sunday doesn't make us better at shepherding people on Monday, then we've missed the point.

From a minister north of the Canadian border comes this observation: "Often in elders meetings the agenda item is stated as 'shepherding concerns.' When we reach that item, the room falls silent. Then the elders will look at me so I can tell them what is going on in the lives of the people."

From Houston a friend writes, "Shepherds have got to love people—I have seen 'shepherds' who want to continue in the boardroom mentality. They do not want to call, visit, or connect with people."

And a president of a Christian university writes, "Shepherds simply must have a heart for people more than for things. To be honest, I have often felt more strongly supported and aided by shepherds who did not wear the formal title. Often the formal shepherds get so wrapped up in flock management that they don't seem to have the time to shepherd individual sheep, and so others sometimes have to step up to fill the gap."

Yet according to the Bible, the grist of Christian shepherding is ground out in the mill of marriages, friendships, partnerships, neighborhoods, communities, property lines, and sales contracts. Sheep are smelly critters, but the shepherd must have the heart to get out there amongst the flock.

Of course, that often gets complicated. Grumpy sheep. Mean ones. Lazy ones. Bosses who demand the impossible. Secretaries who can't perform the minimal. Wives who don't appreciate what wonderful husbands they have. Husbands who think they are too wonderful. Shepherding the flock the Jesus way is no cakewalk. As the old saying goes,

> To live above with those we love,
> > O, that will be glory.
> But to live below with those we know,
> > Well, that's a different story.

SHEPHERD, HOW ARE YOUR RELATIONSHIPS?

Linus, the comic strip character from *Peanuts*, said it for all of us: "I love the world. It's *people* that I can't stand." Yet doing right by people is the shepherd's forte. Our mission is building people. Didn't John say, "For anyone who does not love his brother, whom he has seen, cannot love God, whom he has not seen"?[4]

So we come to an important personal question: Shepherds, how are your relationships? Think for a moment about the people in your flock. Some are in your life by choice: your mate, your best friend, perhaps a business associate. Others you inherited by chance: your relatives, your next-door neighbor, maybe your boss—or the people who make up the church God called you to shepherd. But no matter where you got them, they all have one thing in common: they are people—vulnerable and woundable—who need shepherds who love them unreservedly. Each person matters to God!

Could you use a little help in doing right by people? I guess we all could. And Jesus, the Good Shepherd, can be our trainer . . . if we let him.

My friend Roger calls the people-loving shepherd quality "affability" or "the common touch." And he points to one example:

> One of the most effective examples of shepherding I ever witnessed occurred when a six-foot, four-inch elder named Cecil got down on one knee to show my preteen children how he could wiggle his ears. Years later, my children still recounted that event—when a shepherd took the time to relate to them on their level.

SHEPHERD ON THE WING

Affability is one side of the people-hearted shepherd. My friend Grady describes the other side: empathy.

> Recently my father died. I was in Texas. He was in California. Fathers die; it's life. But the word *father* has not always been easy for me.
>
> My folks divorced when I was eleven. Dad had been a preacher at one time. The ugly divorce gave new meaning to AAA—anger, alcohol, and adultery. When a young boy needed a father with the heart of a shepherd, I felt abandoned, by him and God. I can count on both hands how many times I had been with him since it happened.
>
> I buried my feelings fairly well until age twenty and for the last twenty-nine years have been on a journey of healing and grace. These have come in part through men, with shepherd's hearts, whom God brought into my life—at just the right time.

nine: IT'S ALL ABOUT PEOPLE

I flew to California for Dad's funeral. Not many people showed up at visitation. But then, at just the right time, a very familiar face walked through the doors. It was a Texas shepherd—and one of my best friends—who had dropped me off at the Dallas airport. His presence seized my heart, helped me breathe full breaths again. I didn't realize how much I needed him, till I saw him. He stayed less than twenty-four hours. It wasn't a cheap trip, and he came at the spur of the moment, just days before Christmas. I don't know why I felt so surprised—it is who he is. It was an extraordinary moment of shepherding.

As I told him, "Thanks for coming," he said, "I just had to come. Someone from home needed to be here." Whew! I breathed deeply again, felt friendship and love fill my eyes, and thanked God for the heart of a shepherd.

Contrast this testimony with the blast Ezekiel the prophet unleashed centuries before against unfaithful leaders:

Woe to the shepherds of Israel who only take care of themselves! Should not shepherds take care of the flock? You eat the curds, clothe yourselves with the wool and slaughter the choice animals, but you do not take care of the flock. You have not strengthened the weak or healed the sick or bound up the injured. You have not brought back the strays or searched for the lost. You have ruled them harshly and brutally. So they were scattered because there was no shepherd, and when they were scattered they became food for all the wild animals. My sheep wandered over all the mountains and on every high hill. They were scattered over the whole earth, and no one searched or looked for them.[5]

What a convicting contrast: the judgment of God rests upon neglectful, harsh, self-absorbed, and soul-starving "church officials."

But the blessings of God rest upon attentive, connected, relationship-nurturing, soul-feeding "shepherds." More importantly, their sheep suffer—or flourish—accordingly.

SHEPHERDS AMONG THE PEWS

An old friend, Lewis, writes,

> Two very different types of elders stand out to me. I'll call them "Concerned Clyde" and "Compassionate Cory."
>
> Concerned Clyde would ask me to lunch about once every other month. After the second or third invite, I knew he always wanted me to put out a fire he thought I had lit or share one of his criticisms of my ministry—and tell me who was upset with me now. While I appreciated his time and he was quite often right, I knew that every meeting meant I was in trouble.
>
> Compassionate Cory was the complete opposite. He, too, would often take me to lunch, but he was interested only in me, my family, and my walk. Sometimes he would ask me to identify my struggles, even the mistakes I made. And his compassion as a shepherd was life-changing. Simply put, I knew he cared for me—as a person.

Don, a Dallas business executive, pays tribute to a consummate "people-hearted shepherd" in his church:

> George models the three qualities of heart I most admire: humility, compassion, and selflessness.
>
> As a full-time shepherd, he is paid a modest salary; but you could not pay enough to compensate for what he does. At 6:00 a.m. he may show up at a hospital room for prayer before a critical surgery or late at night for a grieving family. He is usually among the first to see the newborn babies. He sits with the bereaved and

participates in most funerals. His visits are not perfunctory. People know he really cares and, as a result, George forms lasting, trusting relationships.

Follow George around the church on Sunday morning and the scope of his ministry becomes dramatically obvious. Everyone who passes acknowledges his presence with a smile, a hello, and often an embrace. Children, the best judges of heart, run to him and receive a hug. He responds to everyone as a best friend.

George is a true shepherd, and the people know and love his voice. He has a heart for people.[6]

GAINING GOD'S HEART

God's shepherd will have a heart for people because God himself has such a heart. As John Henry Newman penned it:

I sought to hear the voice of God
  And climbed the topmost steeple,
But God declared: "Go down again—
  I dwell among the people."

CARDIOVASCULAR WORKOUTS
FOR SHEPHERD HEARTS

1. Open your calendar. Count the squares over the last three months on which you had "people" scheduled. Now count the ones taken up by "stuff." Write down your reflections when you see the results of your count.

   a. If "people time" exceeded "stuff time":

      • Bow your head, and thank God for what he is doing in your heart.

      • Try to retrace your steps, and put your finger on what led you to make good "people choices."

   b. If "stuff time" exceeded "people time" on your calendar:

      • Bow your head, and ask God for the heart and the discernment to make people "Job One."

      • Try to retrace your steps, and put your finger on what led you to make poor "people choices."

2. What three steps can you take toward becoming more people-oriented?

3. Write down the date and the time you will take the first step.

ten

A HEART FOR LOST AND HURTING PEOPLE

We built a temple, beautiful and tall,
We built it stronger than the Berlin Wall,
We built an altar bright, beneath the belfry
Where we could pray, forgetting hate and poverty
Where we could find a refuge from the heat
Of human anger in the violent street.

There we heard the gentle voice of one who told
Of him who talked of peace in days of old
Calmed were our souls, till it would almost seem
That Calvary was rather like a dream
There we caught in tranquilizing trance,
Could meditate in Holy Arrogance.

We built a ghetto out of shining stone,
Walled in from man, and thus from God
We found ourselves alone.

—Author Unknown

Sundays are easy. The sanctuary is clean and orderly, the symbolism clear, the people polite. I know what I am doing: I am going to lead these people in worship, proclaim God's word to them, celebrate the sacraments . . . I love doing this. I wake up early Sunday mornings, the adrenaline pumping into my veins.

But after the sun goes down on Sunday, the clarity diffuses. From Monday through Saturday, an unaccountably unruly people track mud through the holy places, leaving a mess. The order of worship gives way to the disorder of argument and doubt, bodies in pain and emotions in confusion, misbehaving children and misdirected parents. . . .

Sundays are important—celebrative and essential. . . . But the six days between Sundays are just as important.[1]

So writes Eugene Peterson.

Amen, Mr. Peterson.

It is not so surprising that most real shepherding takes place between Sundays. Nor should it surprise us that God's favorite people—and those heaviest on his heart—are the ones who rarely, if ever, show up at church on Sunday. And the ones who do show up are looking for help, hope, and home: for life resources, for meaning and purpose, for the feeling that things can get better, and for authentic relationships. In other words, they're looking for a place to genuinely belong.

This means that today's churches are best shepherded by leaders who have hearts for hurting people.

GOD'S FAVORITES

Like it or not, "religious folks" are not God's favorite people. However, some religious people in Luke chapter 15 thought they were his favorites. They felt offended that Jesus spent more time hanging out with the riffraff than with them. Knowing their thoughts, Jesus did something he never did anywhere else: he told three stories to make one point.

First story: A man has a hundred sheep. One of them wanders away. He leaves the ninety-nine behind and searches the mountains for the lost one. And when he finds it, he carries the sheep home on his shoulders, shouting, "Let's party. I found my lost sheep!" Then Jesus drove home his point: "Just so, there is a bigger party in heaven over one lost sinner who repents than over all the church folks who feel no need of repentance." Seems as though the riffraff are as dear to God's heart as those who are religious.

That is a *one percent* story. Then Jesus told a *ten percent* story.

A woman lost one of her ten coins. She turned the house upside down looking for it. When she found it, she called out to her friends, "Let's party! I found my coin!" Again Jesus clinched the point: "Just so, a bigger party breaks out in heaven over one sinner repenting, than over all the folks huddled in the church." Why? Because finding lost people makes God happy, and that makes heaven happy!

Then Jesus went for the *fifty percent* story. A man had two boys. One hung around the farm—did his chores, shined his shoes, kept the rules, and made no waves. The other boy rebelled. He didn't like the chores any more than he liked the rules. So he wanted out. As soon as possible he asked his dad for his slice of the estate. Once he got it, he hit the road, singing, "Don't fence me in." But in a short while he had maxed out his credit card on booze and whores. He wound up broke and had to go to work for Gentiles—feeding pigs, of all things (not usually the job good little Jewish boys dream about). He got so hungry, the pig slop started to look appealing.

Then he remembered his dad, came to his senses, and said, "Wait a minute! My dad's hired men are better off by far than me." So he got up and headed toward home, rehearsing a little speech: "Dad, I have really messed up. I know I have no right to be treated like a son anymore. Any chance I could just be a hired man?"

But the boy didn't know what was going on at home. Several times a day his father would drop his tools, step to the gate, and look both ways down the road, hoping to see a familiar figure trudging his way. Each night after dinner his dad would sit on the front porch and wonder, *I hope he is OK. When, oh when, will I see him again?* Then, when darkness fell, his father would stand in the yard, looking up at the house. "There is a light in that window. And a light in that one. But that other window is dark. I wonder where my boy is tonight?"

The boy had no way of knowing what to expect at the gate of the old home place. Before the boy could finish his speech, his father came running to meet him, covering him with kisses and showering him with gifts. "Let's party!" he shouted. "My lost boy is home!"

But the older son didn't get it. He thought he was the favorite child because he had been a "good boy." Resentful, yes; boring, sure—but "good."

This time, Jesus no longer needed to explain his point to his listeners. God favors these with every bit as much love and attention as church folk. Thus the heart of a godly shepherd beats for lost and hurting people.

> The white sheep are placid and graze in quiet places,
> their fleeces like silver that the moon has known.
> But the black sheep have vigor in their ugly faces and
> the best of all shepherds wants them for his own.

ON THE STREET WHERE YOU LIVE

Some in church-leadership positions find it easier and simpler to sit behind closed doors and make decisions about buildings, budgets, personnel, and programs than to deal with troubled people. Spiritual shepherds, on the other hand, might be found at all hours of the day or night:

- in a church member's home, struggling with a marriage about to dissolve

- pouring out a vodka bottle into the kitchen sink

- steering an addict toward recovery

- holding the hand of an unwed teenager who's just found out she's pregnant

My longtime shepherd friend Carlos understands this. Carlos runs a prosperous business. People feel naturally drawn to him because he is always a barrel of fun. Carlos also contagiously loves Jesus. In fact, his faith is so contagious that most nonbelieving people who come to work beside him eventually come to Christ.

"Jan," his bookkeeper, was one of those people. Some years back Jan put her faith in Christ through the ministry of Carlos. She and her husband, "Tom," who was not a believer, hit some rocky times in their marriage. The trouble revolved, as family trouble often does, around finances. They were in debt up to their eyeballs.

One afternoon Carlos felt shocked to discover several thousand dollars missing from his business, covered by phony figures. At first he couldn't believe the culprit was Jan. But the evidence left no other possibility.

I asked Carlos, "What did you do next?"

"Well," Carlos admitted, "first I closed the office door and cried. It really hurt me that it was Jan."

"And then?"

Carlos told how he had called Jan in and confronted her. She didn't deny it. She just began to cry and confess and poured out the details of the financial crisis in her marriage. She hadn't meant to steal. She had given in to temptation and "borrowed" the money, hoping against hope to replace it before anyone found it missing. She asked when Carlos would press charges and said she would clear out her desk immediately.

But Carlos explained there would be no charges. Besides, he said, she wasn't being fired.

"You are my Christian sister, and I want to help you out of this mess," explained Carlos. "I know you are genuinely sorry. All I want is to know that it won't happen again and that you'll pay back the money."

"But there is no way I can pay it back," Jan sobbed. "We couldn't begin to borrow that much with our credit like it is."

Carlos shook his head and explained, "You can pay it back just a few hundred dollars a month, till it's covered—at no interest."

Jan began to cry again, "But even that is impossible! Every penny is gone before I get my check."

"Sure you can," Carlos declared, "when you get your raise." Jan looked at him dumbfounded. Carlos continued: "Starting next week, I'm raising your salary by the amount of your payments."

"Why—why would you do that?" Jan wondered aloud.

"Because I don't want you crushed," Carlos explained. "I want to see you changed and happy and walking with Jesus."

Then Jan and Carlos bowed their heads and prayed together. Jan continued working in Carlos's office as a trusted employee for years afterward and has been a loving follower of Jesus ever since. Plus, Tom eventually became a Christ-follower as well!

Carlos is a shepherd with a heart for lost and hurting people.

ON THE DARK SIDE OF TOWN

I have been privileged to work beside many shepherds who have hearts for God's lost and hurting people. Just one example: Dr. J. M., a marriage and family therapist, was still in recovery from a painful divorce (and rejection by some church leaders) when she first came to our church.

This wounded soul confided to "Sam," one of our shepherds, "I counsel with people every day who are in painful relationships. But as a professional therapist, I cannot open my Bible and talk about the only lasting source of real help. Would it be OK if I could have a room on Wednesday nights to bring people in various kinds of painful relationships? We can operate a bit like group therapy, except I would want to infuse biblical teaching and prayer. And I would like to have elders sit in, just to touch the hurting people and pray for them."

Sam's answer still rings in my ears—and hers: "Dear sister," he replied gently, "did you think you had to have permission to love people around here?"

So began The Challenge Group. It quickly filled a classroom, many participants from nonchurched backgrounds. Then Amy showed up—a tall, attractive woman. Soon she brought her boyfriend, Kyle. Amy and Kyle were both recovering addicts, had met in a bar, loved each other, but fought so much they didn't think marriage could work. But they heard that The Challenge Group could help in painful relationships, so they came.

"Did you think you had to have permission to love people around here?"

Soon Amy began suggesting she needed to quit her job. No one asked why or what the job was. Months later, Amy acknowledged that she worked as a topless dancer; her world overflowed with women in "the sex business." But Amy had made a commitment to Jesus and now saw her body as the temple of the Holy Spirit—and not merely a "marketable asset."

Soon Kyle also gave his life to Christ, and both he and Amy were baptized. A little later, Royce, another shepherd, performed their wedding ceremony.

Amy started bringing friends from her "former world" to The Challenge Group—too many for the space, so a second group was spun out, called Amy's Friends. What a new thing to see several dancers and/ or prostitutes coming into our church, week after week! The shepherd couples not only received and loved them, but served them. Soon they began a 12-step program for Amy's Friends. Each week, elders' wives shepherded these women in prayer, Bible study, and healthy living. Soon a number of the women had been helped to find wholesome jobs. Many of them became Christ-followers. But in the 12-step support groups, the shepherding women treated those of Amy's Friends who were still in the sex business with the very same love and respect as those who already had found wholesome jobs and had become Christians.

These stories amazed the community. Media began to follow this ministry—newspaper coverage, even ABC 20/20. Ten years later, although the ministry has changed names, and Amy stepped away from her leadership role, the ministry is still flourishing and growing today. (Just this morning word came from Amy, "Kyle and I have since divorced. But I am now back as an active member of the same church where I started ten years ago, and I am now raising a beautiful little boy named Jimmy.")

This great rescue ministry began—and continues—because some shepherds had genuine hearts for lost and hurting people.

The hearts of today's shepherds beat with the heart of the Chief Shepherd, the Good Shepherd, who said, "It is not the healthy who need a doctor, but the sick."[2] The best of shepherds long to see lost people found. They search for them and call for them, both outside and inside the church. They equip saved people to love and seek the lost. And they want to shape churches into redemptive "kingdom-rule" communities, repeating this cycle till Jesus comes—because this is the heart of God.

CARDIOVASCULAR WORKOUTS FOR SHEPHERD HEARTS

First, take a pad and pen in hand, then thoughtfully write out your responses to the following:

1. Who is my closest friend, from outside my church, who is lost and hurting?

2. Who is the last hurting and "lost" Christian that came to me as a confidant?

3. When was the last time I approached a lost or hurting person to offer a listening ear and/or a helping hand?

4. What is there about me that might cause a lost and hurting person to feel comfortable around me? What might make them uncomfortable?

5. What next steps could I take toward building a trust relationship with a lost and hurting person?

Next,

1. Write the names of three people you know who are lost and hurting.

2. Pray for each of them.

3. Write down a plan of action you might follow to shepherd each one. Make the plan specific (a separate plan for each person).

4. Write out the first step you could take.

5. Write down the date and time on which you will take that step.

A HEART FOR FOR THE WORD OF GOD

While all Christians need nurture and sustenance, the active Christian leader who encounters spiritual and emotional stress daily has special, urgent needs. If the shepherd is not fed along with the sheep, that inner hunger and fatigue, those unhealed hurts, can cause the shepherd to do great unconscious harm to those within his or her care.

—Flora Slosson Wuellner, *Feed My Shepherds*

eleven

A HEART FOR THE WORD

The shepherd of God's people must never let any lesser chore distract him from giving attention to "the ministry of the word."

—Eugene Peterson

At the dinner table he wanted to impress the new minister, so the elder told his six-year-old, "Son, run and get the big book we read every night." Quick as a flash, the boy came back carrying a copy of *Sports Illustrated*.

Let's be frank: most of us talk more about the Bible than we read from it. Unfortunately, Bibles may be the most-purchased-but-least-read book, even in the homes of some shepherds. In fact, a number of shepherds have shamefacedly confided that they have "never read the Bible all the way through." Instead, they graze on "favorite parts for inspiration and certain verses to support my doctrinal views."

For one to be a true shepherd of the flock, however, he or she must also be "a person of the Book."

TAKE A QUIZ

Shepherd, do you feel confident that you are feeding your flock the right food? That you are counseling the sheep in healthy directions?

Take a little quiz. Pick some point about which you may have strong convictions—say, for example, you believe that Communion should be every Sunday. Now, think quickly: what passage (or verses) would you cite to support this belief? Once you have cited the verse or verses, can you give the chapter context surrounding that verse? If so, can you explain the point of the book in which this chapter is found? And how that chapter contributes to the point of the book? Then can you describe the setting of this book in history, and the place of this book in the overall message of the New Testament?

If this process comes naturally to you, you get a gold star. If you are not able to do this, however, then surely it would not be wise to make a binding doctrine out of your convictions on weekly Communion! You need more than a "proof text." As someone has said, "A text without the context can be a pretext to support a mere prejudice."

The flock you shepherd deserves—and desperately needs—a shepherd with a heart for the Word of God. So hungering to know and teach God's Word is a top priority for shepherds.

FEEDING THE SHEPHERD

Just a few days ago I asked Frank, a shepherd in Tennessee, "Do you still read the Bible all the way through, every year?" And again he assured me, "Yes. I have done that for decades." Frank, like many wonderful shepherds across the country, has a heart that feeds on the Word of God.

Faithful shepherds feed on the Word, because as Frank says, "Even when we 'know it,' we still 'need it.'" Peter says that the point in studying the Bible isn't always to learn something new. More often it is to remind us of something old.[1]

More importantly, reading the Bible leads us repeatedly into an encounter with the awesome God! Last week I couldn't find some old love letters from Carolyn. I rarely take them out to read; why should I, when I have her with me? I would rather have a living conversation with her than have my nose stuck in one of those old letters. The past two weeks, however, she was in Africa, and even out of phone contact. So I wanted to find one of those letters; they had become my vital connection with the one I love.

Just so, in the physical absence of Jesus, the Bible is our love letter that nurtures our relationship with him. The written Word connects us to Jesus.

We have learned what to do with junk mail; it hits the trash, unopened. A magazine might make it to the reading table and a bill to the "to do" box—but a personal letter from someone we know and love? We open that first and read with the utmost relish, more than once, savoring the words. We value the message because we value the sender.

Peter reminds us who "sent" us the Bible.[2] The prophets didn't just dream up this stuff. The pages were written by human pen, yes. But they ultimately came from the mind of God: "Men spoke from God as they were carried along by the Holy Spirit." So we treasure this "mail" because it comes from the One who knows us best and loves us most. He never exaggerates his words of love nor uses them to manipulate us. And his insight and advice is never off target.

FEEDING THE SHEEP

Besides feeding on the Word himself or herself, the shepherd must also have a heart for feeding the Word to the flock. The shepherd who faithfully feeds the flock will make sure that people read the Bible in ways that genuinely help them to see Jesus.

There is a way of reading Scripture, of course, that actually keeps us from approaching God or acknowledging our own perversities—and possibilities. Jesus warned about this:

You diligently study the Scriptures because you think that by them you possess eternal life. These are the Scriptures that testify about me, yet you refuse to come to me to have life.[3]

The shepherd with a heart for the Word uses the Bible to lead his or her flock to encounter the Sovereign One. He longs to help them find light for the journey, to help them manage the day-to-day ethical, moral, and relational challenges of life. He knows that only God's Word supplies a compass able to show people the way in a world of bewildering questions, unbearable sufferings, and profound mysteries, a world without maps explaining how to make it through life's insoluble problems.

Good shepherds have the joy—and the responsibility—to know and to teach the Word.

A SHEPHERD'S PROMISES

A heart-tugging vignette unfolds in the twentieth chapter of Acts. As an aging shepherd, Paul bids a final good-bye to some men who hold a special place in his heart. He has been shepherding them—he had evangelized them, educated them, and also equipped them to shepherd others. And now it is time for him to leave them, never see to them again on this side of heaven.

Yet this was not a day of desperation, but a day of graduation. Paul had worked toward this moment for three years. Now—he was releasing these men to live independent of him, but spiritually dependent upon God.

Faithful shepherds want to leave their sheep strong and self-sustaining when the shepherd can no longer remain among the flock, or when the sheep move out of his sphere of ministry. Paul, too, knew that all relationships end, whether by desertion, divorce, death, or merely by distance. For Paul, this one ended by design. He charges them to move triumphantly beyond the need of his human help. But he leaves them with what they need after he is gone:

> Now I commit you to God and to the word of his grace, which can build you up and give you an inheritance among all those who are sanctified.[4]

Note his charge, phrase by phrase.

First: "I commit you"—calls for responsibility beyond the need of human prodding.

Second: He committed them "to God"—to a relationship not dependent on human personalities.

Third: "And to the word of his grace"—to a guide and resource beyond human counsel. Note that God and his Word are inseparable. This is, after all, the word of his grace!

Fourth: this word of his grace is able to "build you up." God's Word generates life-changing power. I wonder—could Paul have had in mind any of the following power promises from across Scripture? The Word of God:

- Saves[5]

- Enlightens[6]

- Brings faith[7]

- Keeps us from sin[8]

- Probes our very hearts and motives[9]

- Makes us approved in God's sight[10]

- Equips us for good works[11]

- Makes us true disciples[12]

Fifth: this word of his grace is able to "give you an inheritance among all those who are sanctified." In other words, the word of his grace can change the way you die.

What an inheritance, indeed! Our eyes have seen beautiful sights. But we have seen nothing like the panorama that will spread before us when we look at last on "things which [the] eye has not seen."[13]

Scripture says, "His servants will . . . see his face."[14] This is the ultimate end of the "inheritance among all those who are sanctified.

Out of the gathering clouds of the darkness of dying, his face will break through, fresh as a million mornings. His face is "an inheritance among the sanctified." Such is the power of the "word of His grace."

Paul had shepherded these precious friends from Ephesus. He had equipped them in turn to shepherd the flock—and now he committed them to God and his incredibly powerful Word.

Surely this is central to the mission of today's shepherds as well.

With a hunger to know the Word and with a sense of the power of the Word, surely the authentic shepherd will have a heart to teach the Word of God.

IS IT GOSPEL OR CULTURE?
Adapted by Lynn Anderson

As a Christian leader, one must separate the gospel from its cultural barnacles. He or she has no right to de-culturalize the people he or she wishes to reach for Christ. Therefore, the leader must discover what is gospel and instill only this in them.

To recover the core essence of New Testament Christianity, we must hold fast to the "essential" or the "universal" or the "gospel," but also allow freedom and flexibility in matters of culture or nonessentials. Completing the following analysis should help you to begin this crucial process.

SECTION ONE

Listed below are fifty practices and commands that appear in the New Testament. In a sense, all are "scriptural"—that is, they are all in the Bible and are true. The question is, which are meant to be gospel (G) and which are merely cultural (C)? If you have some doubt about which ones belong where, take your time and shift the questionable ones from category to category until you feel more or less satisfied with the result.

Definitions:

GOSPEL means: those elements (commands or precedents) that God wants all people in all ages and in every culture to practice. Whether the item comes before or after conversion, if God wants this done, we shall call it "gospel."

CULTURAL means: those commands or practices present among the people of God, but not by universal command of God. That which

123

is cultural may have some validity in one situation but not in others. God is not necessarily opposed to these "cultural" matters, but they are optional, depending upon the circumstances.

Does that make sense? All right, let's begin. And good luck!

G C   1. Greet one another with a holy kiss. (Romans 16:16)

G C   2. Do not go to law before the unrighteous. (1 Corinthians 6:1)

G C   3. Don't eat meat that has been sacrificed to idols. (Acts 15:29)

G C   4. Be baptized. (Acts 2:38)

G C   5. Wash one another's feet. (John 13:14)

G C   6. Women ought to wear veils on their heads.
         (1 Corinthians 11:10)

G C   7. Give the right hand of fellowship. (Galatians 2:9)

G C   8. Lay on hands (for ordination). (Acts 13:3)

G C   9. It is indecent for a woman to speak in an assembly.
         (1 Corinthians 14:35)

G C 10. Pray at fixed hours ("third hour of prayer"). (Acts 3:1)

G C 11. Abstain from (eating) blood. (Acts 15:29)

G C 12. Abstain from fornication. (Acts 15:29)

G C 13. Observe festivals, new moons, and Sabbaths. (Colossians 2:1)

G C 14. Observe the Lord's Supper. (1 Corinthians 11)

G C 15. The first day of the week begins on Saturday night. (Acts 20:7)

G C 16. Anoint sick people with oil. (James 5:14)

G C 17. I permit no woman to teach men. (1 Timothy 2:12)

G C 18. Prohibit women from wearing braided hair, gold, or pearls.
         (1 Timothy 2:9)

G C 19. Meet on the first day of the week. (Acts 20:7)

G C 20. Preach two by two. (Mark 6:7)

G C 21. Abstain from drinking wine (any potentially intoxicating
         beverage). (1 Timothy 3:8)

G C 22. Speak Greek in the assembly. (the whole New Testament)

G C 23. Eat what is set before you, asking no questions.

   (1 Corinthians 10:2)

G C 24. Own some slaves. (Colossians 4:1)

G C 25. If free from a wife, do not seek marriage. (1 Corinthians 7:27)

G C 26. Be circumcised. (Acts 15:5)

G C 27. Don't eat anything that creeps or any reptile. (Acts 10:12)

G C 28. Have self-employed clergy. (2 Thessalonians 3:7–8)

G C 29. Take formal religious vows. (Paul "shaved his head and took a vow." Acts 18:18)

G C 30. Speak in tongues and prophesy. (1 Corinthians 14:5)

G C 31. Take collections in the assembly. (1 Corinthians 16:1)

G C 32. Meet in homes for the assembly. (Romans 16:23)

G C 33. Wives, be subject to your husbands. (Colossians 3:18)

G C 34. Work with your hands. (1 Thessalonians 4:11)

G C 35. Eat no man's bread without paying for it.

   (2 Thessalonians 3:8)

G C 36. If a man will not work, do not let him eat. (2 Thessalonians 3:10)

G C 37. Lift your hands when praying. (1 Timothy 2:8)

G C 38. Support no widow under sixty years old. (1 Timothy 5:9)

G C 39. Urge younger widows to remarry. (1 Timothy 5:11–14)

G C 40. Pray before meals. (Luke 24:30)

G C 41. Say "Amen" at the end of or during prayers.

   (1 Corinthians 14:16)

G C 42. Fast for spiritual reasons. (Matthew 6:17)

G C 43. Fast in connection with ordination. (Acts 13:3)

G C 44. Use unleavened bread for Communion. (Luke 22:13, 19)

G C 45. Cast lots for church officers. (Acts 1:26)

G C 46. Those who become Christians should sell their property. (Acts 4:37)

G C 47. Owe no man anything. (Romans 13:8)

G C 48. Have seven deacons in any church. (Acts 6)

G C 49. Meet as a church on Saturday. (Acts 13:14, 42, 44)

G C 50. Give to those who beg from you. (Matthew 5:42)

SECTION TWO

Upon which principle(s) did you make your choices?

Now we come to the hard part. Be honest: what is your real principle? It sometimes happens that one will verbalize one principle but actually operate from another. It is not uncommon for one to have a blind spot and thereby not actually be following his or her own stated principle. He or she may be making selections on the basis of pure prejudice.

For example, the principles may be stated something like this: "All commands or practices that _____ are gospel, and all commands and practices that do not _____ are cultural."

Use the bottom of this sheet to write your principle(s) of biblical interpretation.

SECTION THREE

Which of those in your "gospel" list are important enough that you would separate from a church and start a new one if people would not come to your point of view?

Which one(s) would you consider an issue of fellowship?

On the other side of the coin, which of those in the "cultural" list would you tolerate for the sake of the fellowship and unity, even though you would prefer to do things another way?

SECTION FOUR

Naturally, there is no universal agreement among Christians about either the proper principles of biblical interpretation or the specific applications. But consider some questions that help to lead toward developing principles of permanence.

1. Does the context of the whole Bible support or qualify this command?

2. Does the command deal only with a form or is it essential to an underlying meaning?

3. Is the practice actually commanded or merely recorded as a description of what early Christians did?

4. Are the commands related specifically to Jewish life? To Gentile life? To one location? To one situation?

5. Are the commands central to the core of the gospel?

God loves people just as they are,
but he loves them too
much to leave them that way!

—Max Lucado

twelve

THE HEART FOR TEACHING THE WORD

Now the overseer must be . . . able to teach.

—1 Timothy 3:2

Surely every college football fan loved to watch Vince Young work his magic. To see this "rifle-armed, tank-legged, fleet-footed leader of the Longhorns' blitzkrieg offense" stand behind the center, calmly survey the whole field, then either fire his laser-accurate sidearm throw, or glide past defenders with that deceptive long-legged stride. In one year alone, Young earned nearly every possible college football honor, including Heisman runner-up, first-team All-American, and Big 12 Offensive Player of the Year. Young started every game in 2005, completed 212 of 325 passing attempts for 3,036 yards and 26 touchdowns, plus rushed for 1,050 yards and 12 touchdowns. Of course, his crowning achievement was the 2006 Rose Bowl—especially that final spell-binding 8-yard scramble on fourth down for a 41-38 victory over USC—and Texas's first championship in 35 years.

Amazingly, off the field, Young shines just as brightly: community service, mentoring kids in math and science, volunteering at the YMCA, for example, not to mention his warm and respectful people skills—and his whistle-clean life.

However, things were not always this way for Vince Young. His junior-high years found him nursing an attitude and in trouble with the law. He joined the "Bloods" and before long was arrested at a gang fight. From there he may well have ended up in prison, had it not been for a series of positive mentors. Grandma was there early, as was his mother, Felicia—who gave Vince a choice: play football or wash dishes. That was a no-brainer. There Felicia handed the mentoring baton to Coach Seals at Madison High, and in two years Vince was starting quarterback and Seals was shaping him into a wholesome kid. After Coach Seals came Texas coach Mack Brown as well as Tennessee Titans quarterback Steve McNair, who mentored Young some ten years, becoming Vince's godfather in the process. These men polished Young's football skills, of course. But they also continued mentoring Vince into a quality young man of excellent character and high work ethic, and shaping Vince into a follower of Jesus. Vince makes no bones about what got him to where he is: "I can't say enough about the people who have been there for me . . . who cared about the direction I would take and what I would become. Nobody does any of this alone."

JOB ONE

Who hasn't longed for some sort of healthy role model? We naturally tend to become like our role models—even when we don't want to, it seems. This is how human nature works. God has written this principle into our DNA, and that is why it also written into the Bible:

> Appreciate your pastoral leaders who gave you the Word of God.
> Take a good look at the way they live,
> and let their faithfulness instruct you,
> as well as their truthfulness.[1]

Actually, every believer is a mentor, like it or not, either positively or negatively. Most people, at some time in life, define what it means to be a Christian by watching other Christians. But for spiritual leaders, shepherds of God's flocks, mentoring and equipping more spiritual leaders is job number one. This is why the heart of a shepherd burns with a passion for mentoring and equipping others.

This is God's design and how God intends for faith and character to be built into people—one person imitating another person's walk with Christ and one person equipping other persons to equip still others.

Clearly, Jesus led the way in this. And we are to follow. When Jesus gave his "Great Commission," it was to "go and make disciples"[2] (or more literally, "go disciple").

THE GREAT OMISSION

Dallas Willard reminds us, "The followers of Jesus are called Christians only three times in the New Testament. But two hundred sixty-nine times they are referred to as disciples!!!! And a disciple is not a 'Christ-fancier' who merely absorbs a lot of information about Jesus. A disciple is a 'Christ-follower'; an apprentice in the Christ-life. A person whose life is being formed into the likeness of Jesus."[3]

John Ortberg asks, "When we consider divorce rates, addictions, and other behaviors among Christian people, empirically there is not that much difference inside the church from outside. That raises questions: are we really making disciples? Really producing changed people—who in turn change people?"[4]

George Barna would answer Ortberg's questions with a resounding "no." When Barna conducted extensive research regarding the spiritual lives of adults and teenagers who have made a personal commitment to Jesus Christ, he found that the faith commitment of most born-again believers lacks depth.

- Less than 1 percent of all believers perceived a connection between their efforts to worship God and their development as a disciple of Jesus.

- The most widely known Bible verse among adult and teen believers is "God helps those who help themselves"—which is not in the Bible and actually conflicts with the basic message of Scripture.

- Fewer than one out of every ten believers possesses a biblical worldview as the basis for his/her decision-making or behavior.

- When given thirteen basic teachings from the Bible, only 1 percent of adult believers firmly embraced all thirteen as biblical perspectives.

- Most believers stated that their church does little to help them grow as a true disciple.[5]

How do we make disciples? According to Jesus, first we baptize them. And then we teach them "to obey all things I [Jesus] have commanded you." He did not say, "teach them to repeat the sayings I taught you," but to "do what I showed you." Again, *teach* does not mean mere impartation of information. It means training them. It is not merely about information, but about life formation!

This kind of life formation calls for more than an instructor. It calls for a mentor and equipper, a model of the Christ-life, a coach in the Christ-life.

TEACHING AND SPIRITUAL FORMATION

As we have seen, the Bible says shepherds of the church must be "able to teach."[6] The most important kind of teaching, however, often has very little to do with formal Bible classes. In fact, it tends to have much more to do with on-the-job mentoring through sharing life experiences.

This way of making disciples is at the heart of the Great Commission, first modeled and then commanded by Jesus,[7] and subsequently imitated and taught by the apostles.[8]

Surely a shepherd with a heart for the people of God will have a heart for spiritual formation in his flock! I intentionally use the words *spiritual formation* here, rather than just combining *education* and *discipling*. I agree with John Ortberg that some good words can pick up bad baggage. Unfortunately the wonderful New Testament word "disciple" has come to signify some short, time-contained process that one does for a while and then terminates: "Twelve Thursday breakfasts at Cracker Barrel should cover the curriculum."

But the New Testament doesn't use the word in that way. To be a disciple of Jesus involved a process that a shepherd may lead, but which gets worked out in community. It changes everything about us and continues for a lifetime. This kind of discipling addresses the deepest hunger of the soul.

In addition, the words "Christian education" in modern context imply something different from and less than what I mean by "spiritual formation." As Ortberg puts it, "Education is about conveying information, but while information can change people, all you have to do is ask yourself, 'have I ever known somebody that knows ten times more about the Bible than the average person, but is not ten times more loving, or ten times more joyful than the average person?' Information alone isn't enough to transform."[9]

According to George Barna, "Among the barriers to spiritual growth are the tendencies to focus on Bible knowledge (e.g., memorize verses, know the stories of key biblical personalities) but not character development; the lack of a clear and specific idea of what meaningful discipleship is."[10]

The goal of spiritual formation is to change the whole person. God has infinitely more to offer than a few devotional or ministry skills. He wants your life—the whole thing. So spiritual formation is helping people participate in a thoughtful and intelligent and ongoing process of learning to live with Jesus and becoming like Jesus, through everything that goes on in life.

Remember, this kind of spiritual formation or mentoring/equipping was modeled first by Jesus, who built his life into twelve key men, then sent them out to do the same. After them, the great apostle Paul intentionally chose to mentor others. "Whatever you have learned or received or heard from me, or seen in me—put it into practice.[11] He also spelled out his equipping leadership model very simply: "Follow my example, as I follow the example of Christ."[12]

THE BULL'S-EYE

Spiritual formation may look different in modern clothing than it once did, but at its center, we do it now in the same way it was done in the days of Jesus and of Paul. The goal also remains the same: "How does the human person become transformed? How can communities of genuinely loving, joyful, vibrant, alive, winsome, courageous persons be created?"[13]

Paul made it clear that this kind of spiritual formation was not just for Jesus and the apostles. He charged Timothy, one of his "mentees," to "teach these great truths to trustworthy people who are able to pass them on to others."[14]

He also broadened his instructions to include all church leaders. God fitted the church with apostles, prophets, evangelists, and teaching-pastors to equip the sheep "for works of ministry so the flock can build itself up in love." Note: "Equipping of the saints for the work of ministry"[15] or preparing "God's people for works of service"[16] is clearly the bull's-eye of a Christian leader's job description. To put it bluntly, if a Christian leader is not equipping someone to live the Christ-life through works of service, then to that degree that Christian leader is not living up to his or her calling.

Again, the bull's-eye of the spiritual leadership target is making disciples. John Maxwell says, "A success without a successor is a failure."

In growing churches, of course, the paid staff or formal church leaders cannot personally meet all the equipping needs of every Christian. It is rarely possible for these shepherds to personally, intentionally, hands-on equip each willing sheep in his or her flock, especially if the flock is growing rapidly. So God has filled the body of Christ with many potential equippers, besides those who are named as elders or shepherds (or other Christian leaders), to help care for and mentor the needy sheep. I call these "under-shepherds."

If a Christian leader is not equipping someone to live the Christ-life through works of service, then to that degree that Christian leader is not living up to his or her calling.

In many churches the elders or shepherds equip some of these other spiritual leaders, maintaining strong relational connection with the under-shepherd, while the under-shepherd assists the shepherd to care for the sheep. Not all these under-shepherds need to meet the qualifications for elders described in 1 Timothy and Titus. They may be small-group leaders, ministry leaders, prayer partners, Sunday-school teachers, sports-team coaches, or any number of other persons.

In any case, the shepherd with a heart for spiritual formation among the people of God will be intentional, continually expanding the circle of mentors and equippers by equipping others to mentor and equip.[17] Such shepherds will always be scouting for faithful people into whom they can invest their lives, with a view to these people becoming under-shepherds—some of whom may eventually become full-blown shepherds, even if that happens five to ten years down the road.

In one Northeastern church, for example, each elder has been leading a small group for some time. But while doing so, each has also been training under-shepherds, so that now several of these elders lead small groups of small-group leaders, thus killing two birds with one stone. First, they are providing shepherding care for more sheep now through under-shepherds. And second, they are training more elders or shepherds for the future, thus multiplying themselves.

ABLE TO TEACH

Let me repeat: when the Bible says that shepherds must be "able to teach," it likely isn't referring primarily to classroom instruction, but to life formation. A good example of a shepherd with a heart for the Word came from my friend Gary. He writes:

> Thirty years ago Patti and I were newlyweds. I had taken her to live at the end of the earth, Albuquerque, NM. I was still a hippie, sucking down pot, and looking for a fight from those hypocritical church folks.
>
> But George and Angie just sort of showed up in our lives. George was a nuclear physicist. Yeah, he could talk over your head, but he never did. Then, they seemed more like in-town parents. Now, we consider them to have been incredible shepherds.
>
> They were always just, well . . . "there." We would get a quick call on a Friday or Saturday night, "Hey, we're just now throwing some burgers on the grill. Why don't you guys come on over, and we'll eat and play some cards and visit a spell."
>
> When we bought our first house we couldn't afford (for $39,000), they encouraged us to be wise stewards, building equity instead of paying rent. "Remember that your new house is really God's. Use it for him. Practice love and hospitality with what he has given you."
>
> "No, you don't need to pay to have a sprinkler system put in, we can do that together. Come on over, and we'll lay that dude out and make a materials list."
>
> "When?"

"How 'bout tonight?"

And every practical learning opportunity was salted with spiritual overtones, applications, or just straight up, look-you-in-the-eyes biblical teaching.

When our first son came along, I was standing with my nose pressed against the glass of the hospital nursery when, all of a sudden, old George was there beside me, pressing his face against the glass next to mine. The glass in front of our faces got all foggy about the same time as he whispered, "Don't ever forget these moments. What a miracle from God you've just been a part of! How he delivered you and your wife (Patti almost died) and your new son. Watch what he will do in the life of this baby boy of his and yours. First sons. Amazing, isn't it? Remember the story of Abraham and Isaac, how . . ."

"By the by, don't ever call Patti, 'Mom.' She's not your mother; she's your wife. She's your best friend. She's your lover."

The day finally came when it was time to say good-bye to George and Angie. We had delayed this one as long as possible. It was so hard to breathe because the lumps in our throats had to be as big as softballs.

Angie was bawling like us. George was choking 'em back, too, when he put his arm around my shoulder and said, "Let's walk a little bit," and led me down the driveway and away from our wives.

I wanted to thank him so much, but there didn't seem to be words enough or right enough to express what I was feeling. He seemed to know that. So he took over.

"Gary, you are going to be a very good and sensitive shepherd some day. God will be preparing you all along the way. Watch where you walk. Consider even all the difficult times in your life as God is equipping you to be a leader. When the time is right for you to serve the church as a shepherd, he'll let you know. He will have put many people in your life to prepare you, and he will keep people in your life, always teaching you, equipping you, mentoring you.

"And always, always, share what you have been taught."[18]

George and Angie were shepherds with hearts for teaching the Word of God. And their teaching paid off! Now, decades later, Gary and Patti effectively mentor some of God's flock in Denver and are in turn equipping some of their sheep to become shepherds.

CALLING ALL MESQUITES

Remember, this book is about mesquite bushes, not about banyan trees. God calls very few Banyan Tree leaders—visionaries who stand alone and lead movements. Mostly, God calls the Mesquite Bush kind of spiritual leaders. These leaders do not necessarily stand out against the sky, but they keep multiplying themselves by producing healthy, growing, reproducing disciples of Jesus.

What better legacy could any Christian leave behind than an expanding circle of spiritual formation specialists who keep multiplying themselves through the lives of others? What could possibly be more rewarding? Let me challenge you, dear reader, to consider Mesquite Bush leadership as your life's mission.

CARDIOVASCULAR WORKOUTS
FOR SHEPHERD HEARTS

My friend Rick Brown says, "*Incremental* goals urge us to do more, better, harder, etc. of the same things. But *transformational* goals have to do with doing things we have not been doing that, if we did them, would move us toward our goal faster. We are looking for 'a vision path toward transformational goals and strategies.'"

To establish and fulfill transformation goals:

First, clearly identify the gap between "current reality" and "God's preferred future" in the disciple-maturing and equipping strategies in your church. Then, do the same for your own spiritual leadership strategies.

Second, clearly identify ways to create a vision path to close the gap between the two. God shows us where those gaps are, not for our condemnation but for our transformation.

Third, in light of the above:

1. Find a complete list of members who have joined your church in the past two to three years.

2. Put a check mark beside the name of each person you know. (Remember, this is not about condemnation but about transformation.)

3. Put a star by each name where you know which shepherd is caring for that sheep.

4. Write down the names of three people you might help disciple to maturity.

5. Write down the date you will begin equipping the first of these three people.

Finally, pray daily for the Lord to show you and your fellow shepherds the healthiest and shortest route to multiplying the number of shepherds and under-shepherds needed to take care of the harvest God is bringing.

Your word is a lamp to my feet and a light for my path.

—Psalm 119:105

thirteen

KEEPERS OF THE FOREST

The things you have heard me say . . . entrust to reliable men who will also be qualified to teach others.

—2 Timothy 2:2

Max Lucado sat at an elegant dinner beside a man from Germany. To make conversation, Max asked the German gentleman what he did for a living. The German responded, "I am the keeper of the forest."

"Oh," probed Max, "and what does a keeper of the forest do?"

"Put simply," the gentleman responded, "I harvest the trees my father planted. And I plant the trees my sons will harvest. So I must always plant more trees than I harvest."

What an eloquent metaphor for the heart of the shepherd: *a heart for spiritual formation among the people of God.* May all who came before us find us faithfully living out the legacy of faith they left us. And at the same time may we mentor and equip a generation of faithful men and women who come after us. To do that, may we multiply and leave behind us more well-equipped and faithful persons than we have found!

Bottom line: our mission is to make disciples who will make still more disciples who make still more.

TREES ALL OVER

The good news is that real, live "keepers of the forest" are planting trees all over the world today. Here are the stories of just a few.

1. James and Marie

James and Marie of Tennessee are keepers of the forest. Their daughter, Anne, reminded me how her parents kept the faith alive, first in their children and then in their grandchildren:

> Mama and Daddy went from Tennessee to Mississippi to visit last week (not bad for a couple aged eighty-six and eighty-eight).
>
> But what I realized last week is really special. Charlie's son, Tom (grandson), was installed as a deacon in his home church. Richard Brown (a grandson) is teaching at a Christian university and doing campus ministry for a nearby church.
>
> Scott (grandson) is a deacon and "leader-in-training" at a church in Massachusetts. Andy (a grandson) is a deacon in a Maryland church. Ethan (a grandson) is a minister in Massachusetts. Tom (son) is a deacon in Tennessee.
>
> That means that all five of Mama and Daddy's grandsons/grandsons-in-law are working hard in their home churches, in leadership roles of one sort or another. I'm guessing there are very few couples today who could make that claim.
>
> Of course, if you throw in (son) Charlie, who ministers to everybody, and Joe (son), who is primo song leader and caretaker for most of the old people in the county, it's pretty easy to see that Mama and Daddy had a strong influence on a lot of young men and women.
>
> They wouldn't claim anything like that, because they think it's just the way it's supposed to be!

Obviously, part of "the forest to be kept" is our own families, so we "leave more tress than we found."

thirteen: KEEPERS OF THE FOREST

2. Cory

Of course, a lot of trees must be planted beyond our own families. Cory is a keeper of one of these "extended forests". He has been a church elder since before he was forty, but has no passion for management or extended policy meetings. His passion is shepherding and equipping.

Cory leads a "life-talk" luncheon once a month with people in his workplace. This luncheon gathers a mixture of people: agnostics, Muslims, Buddhists, as well as people from various Christian denominations. They simply read through the Bible together and then talk about life.

Cory also leads a special mentoring/equipping "little flock" from his church. These are mostly new Christians, working themselves free from lifelong sin habits, and learning how to be godly mates, parents, and friends. This multiracial, multiethnic collection of pilgrims meets Wednesday mornings for study, prayer, and accountability. Periodically they also go on weekend retreats, like a recent one to a west Texas mountain ranch called "a retreat on your feet," a weekend of hiking, Bible study, prayer, and bonding. Cory and his wife, Sue, also arrange a good deal of social time together with these people and their spouses. Cory believes many of these mentees will one day shepherd others, maybe even become elders of the church.

Cory intends to "leave more trees than he found."

3. Gerald

The late Gerald Jackson was also a keeper of the forest. When Gerald passed away, his wife, Ruth, asked my son Jon to give a eulogy. Jon was unable to attend in person, so he wrote the following to be read at the memorial.

Gerald Jackson—Mr. Jackson to me—was my wood-shop teacher in ninth grade. As most people know, one of the hardest things to manage is a ninth-grade boy. Now, as a forty-two-year-old man,

I love to work with wood. I imagine Jesus when he was about fourteen years old, working with his father and being taught many lessons of life while learning to mold crude pieces of wood into useful and beautiful things. Mr. Jackson was that kind of teacher to me.

In ninth grade Mr. Jackson challenged us to design and build our own wood creation. I took this very seriously. For some reason Mr. Jackson convinced me that he believed in me. I set my sights on a cedar curio box, complete with a tight-fitting, hinged lid. Mr. Jackson didn't bat an eye, but went about encouraging me to make it as intricate as I wanted. I still have that box, and it holds many important pieces of childhood memorabilia.

That summer, Mr. Jackson offered me my first full-time job, helping him build his new house. I don't know if he realized it, but getting that job was my initiation into manhood. Before that, the closest thing I had ever had to a job was cutting lawns. This time someone actually believed in me enough to let me help build the house that they were going to live in. The way he taught me was masterful, although I didn't know it at the time. Every weekday morning I would show up at the site, and he would start me working on something with him.

After an hour or so of assisting him, he would trade places with me and become my assistant—for an hour or two. Then he would say he was going up the hill to his apartment to do some chores, and that I should come get him when I was finished. For some reason I always seemed to have just enough work to get done by lunchtime, and then I would go up to the apartment where he would have a sandwich waiting for me. Funny how certain people impact you in such a big way, but you can't remember a single thing they said. That's how lunchtime was: I'm sure we did plenty of talking, but I don't remember a word of it. After lunch we would go back to building and, again, he would get me started on something and then leave me to finish it.

Throughout my adult life I have often come upon situations where I was asked to handle something I have never done before. A few years later, while working for a landscape company, one day the boss asked if anybody knew how to run a backhoe. I barely knew what *backhoe* meant, but I raised my hand. The boss threw me the keys and told me to go bring it from the other side of the building. Off I went and, although I didn't figure it out right away, it wasn't terribly long before I came around the corner, proudly smiling and driving the backhoe.

A couple of years ago I was asked to run a program at a community college in which I would be in charge of a staff of more than thirty people, which included several with master's and doctoral degrees. I would never have dreamed I could take on such a responsibility if God had not put Mr. Jackson in my life back in the summer of ninth grade. Even more important than teaching me confidence, I learned from Mr. Jackson that God can use us best when we don't look for ways to bring glory to ourselves, but when we lovingly and quietly help others to grow.

Obviously, Gerald Jackson was more than a shop teacher. He was a shepherd. He was a keeper of the forest—and left my son "planting more trees."

FACES OF FUTURE FORESTS

You, too, can be a keeper of at least some small acre of the forest. In fact, if you let your church call you an elder, you *must* be a "forest keeper"! Whether you are a man or a woman, young or old, it is never too soon—or too late—to start helping empower people for better living. Plant some trees! You may even plant far more trees than you harvested. It's worth it!

Margaret Everts was a quiet keeper of the forest. The daughter of a pastor, Margaret married a young Minneapolis attorney, Elisha Mears, in 1869 and moved to Minneapolis. Her pastor there said of her: "She literally reveled in the Word of God. . . . As a Bible teacher she had few equals in the city of Minneapolis."

Margaret's youngest daughter, Henrietta, would find her mother in prayer early every morning and resolved to follow her footsteps. When Margaret died in 1910, Henrietta "harvested the trees her mother had planted" and began planting a whole new forest. Henrietta Mears went on to become Christian education director at First Presbyterian Church in Hollywood and one of the most widely influential Bible teachers of her day. She led hundreds of young people to enter full-time ministries. Among the people Henrietta influenced were Bill Bright (Henrietta encouraged Bright as he launched Campus Crusade for Christ), Jim Rayburn—Young Life, Richard Halverson—Senate Chaplain, Louis Evans Jr.—the Hollywood Group, Chuck Swindoll, and Billy Graham. In fact, Billy Graham called Henrietta Mears "one of the greatest Christians I have ever known."

> Who knows what world-changer is waiting right around your next corner.

The vast forests all these forest keepers have planted defies even imagination! Margaret Everts may have had no idea she was planting such a mammoth future forest—or any forest at all. But she faithfully planted. And Henrietta faithfully harvested Margaret's small grove, and God since turned that into a global forest of world-changers. And had you or I visited Henrietta Mears routine Bible circle, we may have looked into the upturned faces of those young people and seen nothing more than an ordinary, yawning study group. But God saw the likes of Bill Bright, Jim Rayburn, Richard Halverson, Louis Evans Jr., Chuck

Swindoll, and Billy Graham—plus thousands more. Who would have thought it!

Dear shepherd, What could possibly be more important than spiritual formation and equipping? When you and I look into the faces of the people in our circles of influence, especially the children, what do we see? This very day, might you be looking into the face of the next Moses or Paul or Luther or Rick Warren, or a Max Lucado or Rick Atchley or Bob Russell or Bill Hybels or Mother Teresa? Who knows what world-changer is waiting right around your next corner.

Maybe it is not a child at all. Not even an eager young Bible student. It may, instead, be that ragged sheep that is part of your flock—and God is waiting for you, the shepherd, to mentor and equip him or her to be a future world-changer.

Maybe it's the tattooed, pierced guy talking that horrible "street" lingo stuff: Who knows—he might be an incredible leader someday.

Or that teen who seems totally out of control? He never minds his parents; he lies all the time; he won't stay within the boundaries.

Maybe even that flashy single-parent mom who acts like an opportunistic slut looking for a man. God might choose to use any one of them.

Of course, chances are, you may not produce a Christian Heisman winner or Rose Bowl quarterback or famous evangelist or author—but then, who knows? Maybe without being aware of it, you may quietly help shape the heart of God's next major world-changer! At the very least, you will likely encourage some struggler and help turn a life around—keep at least one more tree alive for the future.

CARDIOVASCULAR WORKOUTS
FOR SHEPHERD HEARTS

1. Build a GGTW list (Guys & Gals to Watch).

2. Write down the names of specific persons in whom you see a teachable spirit and who might want you in their life.

   a. Begin praying daily.

   b. Pray that God will help you see who they really are.

   c. Then pray for the right way and time to pull up beside them. Don't hurry the process! Pursue God's timing. It may take months for your list to take shape. And it may even take a year or two for the connection with these persons to come about.

   d. But keep praying for them and for yourself.

3. These questions might help you as you shape your list:

   a. Who am I mentoring now?

   b. Who could I mentor or shepherd more intentionally and effectively?

   c. Which of the people coming to mind seem to have the most teachable spirit, willing heart, and evident gifts?

   d. How do I discern a teachable spirit?

   e. What changes might I make in my GGTW list because of this reflection?

   f. Who do I know that is going through similar trials as mine, to whom I could provide hope?

   Pray that God would show these individuals to you.

THE HEART
OF A
SERVANT

*For this is what the Sovereign LORD says: I myself will
search for my sheep and look after them. As a shepherd
looks after his scattered flock when he is with them,
so will I look after my sheep. I will rescue them from
all the places where they were scattered on a day
of clouds and darkness. I will bring them out from
the nations and gather them from the countries,
and I will bring them into their own land.
I will pasture them on the mountains of Israel,
in the ravines and in all the settlements in the land.*

—Ezekiel 34:11–13

fourteen

A HEART
WITH HANDS

You know how much of a servant you are
by the way you act when you are treated like one.

—Gene Wilkes

George Washington often signed his letters, "Your most humble and obedient servant." No offense, Mr. President, but do you really expect us to believe *that*? We've grown cynical about such claims. We know lots of people—even good churchgoing, religious people—who:

- use one another

- compete with one another

- undermine and discredit one another

- even combat one another

Sadly, we know precious few who authentically *serve one another*. The word *servant* has all but lost its content. Besides, we pay little attention to words anymore. We walk through a blizzard of them. Over 140,000 book titles per year are published in America.[1] At average reading speed, reading twenty-four hours a day, it would take seventeen and a half years just to read one year's output. And then there's radio, television, and the Web!

We all feel overwhelmed. So tell me, what real chance does a quiet, homely word like *servant* stand in such a cynical and word-saturated environment?

I think God must have seen this coming and that is why he gave us more than a word. Instead, he made a house call and demonstrated a servant heart right here at our address.

THE ALMIGHTY ON HIS KNEES

Here is the way it started:

> [Jesus Christ] who, being in very nature God, did not consider equality with God something to be grasped, but made himself nothing, taking *the very nature of a servant*, being made in human likeness.[2]

And here is the way it ended: at the close of John's Gospel, Jesus gathers His loved ones to demonstrate to them the servant role in high drama. To set the stage, John the narrator points out that Jesus is on his way to the cross. "Jesus knew that the time had come for him to leave this world."[3] He had "come from God and was returning to God."[4] Then . . . the curtain rises.

- Jesus "got up from the meal"—as he had left his throne in heaven's glory.

- He "took off his outer clothing"—as he had stripped himself of his heavenly glory.

- He "wrapped a towel around his waist"—as he had wrapped himself in our humanity.

- "He poured water into a basin and began to wash his disciples' feet"—as he had died to bring us cleansing and forgiveness.

- "He put on his clothes and resumed his seat"—as he has taken his place again in glory at the right hand of God.

Finally, Jesus turned to the audience and drove home the punch line. "Listen, I am more than your Savior. I am your Teacher and Lord." As much as to say, "I have dwelt in unapproachable light. I spoke the universe into existence. My footprints mark the Milky Way. But I am a servant. And if you are to follow me, you must be servants, as well."

His disciples must have been thunderstruck. The rabbis could expect their students/disciples to carry their belongings, maybe even pay some of their bills. But wash their feet? Unthinkable! That is the work of a slave.

But all of history stops to ponder the scene: God Almighty on his knees, with a towel in his hands, doing slave labor. And who then said, *I want you to do as I have done. If I washed your feet, you must wash each other's.*

In this, no Christian is at liberty to disagree with or disobey the Master. The glory of God compels us, above all things, to be genuine servants of one another. Every day.

THE COST OF CREDIBILITY

Servanthood puts teeth in our teaching. For the world to see Christians authentically serving them and serving one another cuts through cynicism and over-communication like no words ever could.

Caitlin, our twenty-year-old granddaughter, is a prenursing student who spent most of last year doing first-aid medical missions in Africa. A very encouraging note regarding her service came to us from Marsha, Caitlin's coworker and mentor.

It seems that Sayon II and some Muslim friends greeted an Arab Muslim teacher on the street. As frequently happens between Arabs and Africans, the Africans were snubbed. As they walked on, the Muslims said to Sayon, "See, this is why Islam is not more successful here. It cannot exceed the level of our teachers." Sayon responded by saying, "There is a young Christian woman in our village who welcomes sick people, washes their filthy sores with her hands, and bandages them and sends them away with a smile."

That is what makes Caitlin effective. It's the Jesus in her. Actions and attitudes communicate when words cannot.

Francis of Assisi said, "Wherever you go, preach the gospel. *If necessary, use words!*" We preach most credibly through service.

DO-GOODERS VERSUS SERVANTS

The terrain can become tricky here, however. There is a life-and-death difference between pity and compassion. *Pity* suggests distance, even a certain condescension. Sometimes I find myself acting with pity. I give some money to a beggar at a stoplight. But I do not look him in his eyes or sit down and talk with him. *Compassion* means to become close to the one who suffers. To say, "I cannot give you a solution for your problem, but I can promise you that I won't leave you alone."

There is also a difference between real servants and mere self-righteous "do-gooders." In his book *Celebration of Discipline*,[5] Richard Foster draws this contrast. Let me summarize the heart of Foster's contrast but using my term "Do-gooders" in place of Foster's term "self-righteous service":

Do-gooders gravitate toward big things—because they make the doer appear big. *Servants*, however, do what needs to be done—no matter how menial the task.

Do-gooders always have one eye on the reward. If the affirmation and applause is not forthcoming, enthusiasm declines. *Servants* delight in hiddenness and in anonymity. They serve for the love of serving.

Do-gooders are preoccupied with results. They study statistics, make comparisons. *Servants* just serve. They do not serve so that their peers call them successful, but so God should count them faithful.

fourteen: A HEART WITH HANDS

Do-gooders pick and choose whom they will serve. They serve folks they enjoy being around, folks who will be "real trophies." They pick those who can reciprocate. The "Jesus style" servant, however, is servant of all. You observe this by the ones he or she spends time with: the lonely, the rejected, the disabled, the helpless, and the disenfranchised—not just "beautiful people."

The *do-gooder* serves when he or she feels like it. The *servant* serves whenever there is need: helping others to function regardless of moods and feelings. "Most of the good that is done in this Old World is done by folks who don't feel like it at the time," says Wendell Broom.

The basin and towel are within our reach. They are something I can reach. *Anybody* can be a servant. It doesn't take scholarship. It doesn't take gifted preaching. It doesn't take looks, brains, or talent to get in on the action. Not even money! Think about it: *"The wonderful thing about what God wants most is that anybody can do it."*

THE POWER OF TOUCH

Sometimes service is as simple as a human touch. A quick survey of the Gospels shows us that Jesus reached out his hands to touch many people. One was a leper who came begging to be healed. Jesus, "filled with compassion . . . reached out his hand and *touched* the man . . . [and said,] 'Be clean!'"[6]

Unthinkable in Jesus's day! Leprosy was considered a curse, the result of sin, highly contagious, and always fatal. So, touch a leper and soon you will begin the ugly process of dying your own slow, horrible death—as an outcast sinner.

Yet Jesus *touched* this man! He could have healed him without touching him. He had healed others from a distance of miles away. But this man needed a healing beyond leprosy alone. He needed someone to touch him. To give him a human touch was to offer acceptance, the assurance that he mattered to someone. Sometimes the hands of a servant-hearted disciple offer nothing more than a touch; but there is, as we all acknowledge, tremendous power in a simple human touch.

Back when AIDS first surfaced, it looked like the modern-day equivalent of ancient leprosy. People assumed AIDS resulted from sin, was highly contagious, and was fatal in a slow, horrible way. Many believed that if you touched a person with AIDS, you would likely be infected—and eventually you would die of it.

The first person I knew with AIDS once asked me to put my arm around him and pray for him. It was not a homosexual request. It was a *human* request. This was back in those early days of HIV awareness, and I felt terrified. But somehow I mustered the courage to put my arm around him and pray.

As soon as I touched him, he began to sob. "That is the first time another human being has touched me in more than a year," he explained. "Except a doctor with rubber gloves on." My hug held healing power! No, not healing of the physical illness. But healing of the emotional, spiritual illness of alienation and aloneness.

There seems to be something very special about the power of touch. Perhaps this is why Scripture speaks of elders praying over the sick, anointing them "with oil in the name of the Lord."[7] The power may not be so much in the oil, as in the touch.

A former minister, Roger, told me the following story.

There was a moment in my life when I badly needed a shepherd's touch—and I received it. When my wife of twenty-eight years decided to end our marriage, the pieces of my life fell like so many dominos. Within a month's time I lost my marriage and my ministry. I had to rent out my house to keep from losing it, which left me, for all practical purposes, homeless.

I moved into a spare bedroom at the home of my son and daughter-in-law and set out to put the pieces of my life back together. Despondent and only marginally employed, I began receiving counseling from a wonderful Christian psychologist who was a member of the church I was attending.

After some weeks he suggested that I meet with the elders of the church, asking them to bless me. This sounded novel to me. I would discover that this was routine with those shepherds.

The next Wednesday night I told my story to the elders. All sixteen of them gathered around me and laid hands on me, asking God to bless me. It was a marvelously healing moment. The tender touch of my shepherds played a large role in the healing of my soul.

HELPING HANDS

Many people, of course, need more than a single touch of a shepherd's hands. They need acts of practical service, helping hands that do work on their behalf.

I'm glad to report that there are still plenty of real servants walking our streets. You would have to hunt a long time to find shepherds more servant-hearted than John and Evelyn Willis. Although John is a world-class Old Testament scholar, neither he nor Evelyn seek the limelight. Both are quiet, humble servants who always greet everyone with a warm smile and an encouraging word.

A few weeks ago our granddaughter Andress graduated from college. At the ceremony, our family sat with John and Evelyn. As student after student crossed the platform to receive a diploma, Evelyn or John not only knew the name of each student, but knew most of their stories, remarking on the achievements of each and adding little personal vignettes. Most of those students had often been in the Willis home. Every Sunday night, for more than thirty years, John and Evelyn have cooked chili or pizza for a houseful of homesick college students.

At the graduation ceremony, our son-in-law Randy (Andress's father) recalled that John Willis was also the first person at the hospital the morning Andress was born; and now, twenty-one years later, here John was again, sitting with us at her graduation. We couldn't help observing aloud that many other families could tell a similar story about the Willis family.

I ministered with John's church for nearly twenty years, and I rarely recall visiting the hospital room of a desperately ill person, or the home of a bereaved family, where John and Evelyn were not there—usually long before me. And they were at a lot more places where I never showed up.

John and Evelyn are servant-hearted shepherds; the kind God-hungry people want to be like.

A friend in Montana tells about another servant-hearted shepherd team:

> Marvin is now seventy-three years old. He and his wife, Darlene, serve Denny, who suffers from MS. Denny's marriage ended in divorce while his MS was destroying his body. When he became confined to a motorized cart, Marvin and Darlene offered to clean Denny's house. Denny declined, not wanting to be a bother. So while Denny was at work, Darlene and Marvin (handyman that he is) "broke into" Denny's house, stripped beds, did the laundry, cleaned the whole house, remade the beds—generally made the house perfect. Denny was speechless. More amazing, they now do this every week! Plus, they have trained and mobilized a whole team specifically to care for Denny.

The stories go on, including two widows, Alene Treece in her 80s and June Chrisner in her 70s, who call every shut-in of their large church every Thursday. And Bill Nash, a recovering alcoholic, hauling van loads of people in wheelchairs to church and leading dozens of twelve-step groups. Or Jim McQuiggin, in Ireland, nursing his completely helpless, bedfast wife, twenty-four hours a day, year after year.

And for fifty years I have witnessed the quiet servant heart of my wife, Carolyn, filling our house with guests of all ages. Hundreds of baby and bridal showers. Food to sick neighbors. Buying my clothes and packing for every trip. Holding the head of young men dying with AIDS. Bringing a drunken church teenager to our house, cleaning up her vomit and nursing her back to soberness. These are servants. And any of us can do what they do.

ROOM FOR ALL

The landscape of service is huge, with room for all of us. Choose your little corner and get busy.

There is the service of small things—a cup of cold water or caring for the neighbor's dog while they are on vacation.

The service of guarding the reputation of others—not only by expecting and saying only the best, but also by refusing to participate in negative conversations about "George" in his absence. Having the courage to say, as one shepherd does frequently, "What did George say when you spoke to *him* about that?"

There are ministries of courtesy, hospitality, burden bearing—the world cannot contain the list. There is *always* a way to serve. No shepherd need ever say, "Wish I could find a way to be of service to someone."

One shepherd-hearted person wrote the following prayer for all shepherds:

Lord, help me live from day to day,
    in such a self-forgetful way,
        that even when I kneel to pray,
            my prayers will be for others.

Others, Lord, yes others.
    May this my motto be.
        Help me to live for others,
            That I might live like thee.

CARDIOVASCULAR WORKOUTS
FOR SHEPHERD HEARTS

1. Pull together two friends, and tell the stories of two or three servant-shepherds who have touched your life.

2. Discuss differences between "servants" and "do-gooders."

   a. How does one spot "do-gooderism" in oneself?

   b. How does one cultivate a genuine servant heart?

3. Write down the names of three people you might be able to serve at this point in your life and how you can serve them.

4. Write down the date, place, and act of service you will do for the first of these three persons.

fifteen

A BROKEN HEART

The man who has not suffered, what does he know anyway?
—Rabbi Abraham Heschel

John Ortberg said, "We did a survey at our church and asked thousands of people, 'Think about an era in your life when you felt like you were growing the most spiritually.' The number one answer: Pain! Pain has a way of opening people up to God."[1] So it stands to reason that the best shepherds often are those with broken hearts.

And hearts get broken in several ways.

BROKEN BY THE SHEEP

Sometimes a shepherd's heart gets broken by the very sheep he loves so much. But why should this surprise us? Jesus, the Chief Shepherd,[2] said it would be so. Jesus was himself "a man of sorrows, and familiar with suffering."[3] And he said that this would be the way of all shepherds, indeed of all Christ-followers: "'No servant is greater than his master.' If they persecuted me, they will persecute you also."[4]

My friend Gene Wilkes observes, "A follower of Jesus Christ who seeks to lead like Jesus must be willing to be treated like Jesus. Some will follow. Others will throw stones."

Getting hurt by those we attempt to shepherd is not merely one of the hazards of the trade; it is inevitable. In fact, getting hurt is *the central means by which the best ministry gets done.* If you don't love someone deeply enough that they can hurt you, you likely don't love them enough to do them much good.

The specific point in all of human history when the most ministry got done in the shortest amount of time occurred that afternoon when a man hung in the darkness on a cross and screamed out with a loud voice, "My God, my God, why have you forsaken me?"[5] At times, those who lead others in following Jesus will be constrained to absorb hostility without retaliation, without complaint, and without bitterness. Jesus even called this kind of pain a "blessing":

> Blessed are those who are persecuted because of righteousness, for theirs is the kingdom of heaven. Blessed are you when people insult you, persecute you and falsely say all kinds of evil against you because of me.[6]

But someone says, "No, no, no! That is too vulnerable. People might take advantage of you. You can get hurt."

Exactly. Sometimes that is what it means to follow "a man of sorrows and familiar with suffering." Surely when we invest our souls into other people, we might quite literally "work through grief," as James Dittes described it:

> To grieve is to take two coffee cups from the cupboard in the morning, only to remember she left last month . . . and to have to put one cup back. . . .
>
> To grieve is to be delighted with the snapshot prints and impulsively to order duplicates for Mother, only to remember that

she died six months previously . . . and to say to the clerk, "Never mind."

To grieve is to pour one's energies for months and years into the struggles of a beleaguered minority group or a beleaguered marriage or a beleaguered teenager, only to have the group or couple or teenager, having found themselves, shun you as a threatening reminder. Or they don't even remember.[7]

Most people experience this kind of grief two or three times in a lifetime: the grief of a promise broken by a trusted parent or teacher, or being jilted by a lover, divorced by a spouse, betrayed by a friend. But a brokenhearted shepherd may well "experience this kind of grief two or three times in a single week."[8] When we walk beside broken people, our own souls can be broken.

Yet what many Christ-followers need about as much as anything else are flesh-and-blood models of suffering love, walking ahead of them—or even better, beside them.

That's my soul lying there.
You don't know what a soul is?
You think it some flimsy, sheet-like thing that you can see through
And that floats on air.
So it's my soul lying there.
Remember the time I got nervous in the group and talked too much.
Well I was putting my soul on the line.
Remember the time I lost my temper, made a fool of myself,
I was putting my soul on the line that time too.
That's my soul lying there:
You can pick it up if you want to. That's why I put it there.
Or you can ignore it if you want, and it will go away
Or you can manhandle it and it will bruise and
turn rancid like an old banana.

But if you'll put your soul there beside it,
You might find love.
You might even find God.[9]

BROKEN BY DIVERSITY

Sometimes a shepherd's heart gets broken by the very diverse and unrealistic expectations of the church. And no matter how attentive and creative a shepherd may be, he cannot live up to everyone's expectations. Consequently, thin-skinned, insecure shepherds won't lead well or last long.

The durable shepherd must at times bear the pain of choosing to listen to the voice of Jesus rather than to the clamor of the crowd. In his letter to Corinth, the apostle Paul makes this clear to Christian leaders:

> So then, men ought to regard us as servants of Christ and as those entrusted with the secret things of God. Now it is required that those who have been given a trust must prove faithful. I care very little if I am judged by you or by any human court; indeed, I do not even judge myself.[10]

The specific term for *servant* Paul uses here describes the slave chained in the galley of a ship, with an oar in his hands. These "under-rowers" pulled the oars to the cadence called out by their master. His voice alone controlled them. They ignored the cacophony of other voices on deck. So Paul says the Christian leader must prove "faithful" to his Master, and therefore should be judged only by the master's expectations, not by anyone else's expectations—not even his own.

I have watched up close as shepherds agonized as they listened for the cadence of the Master's voice—while folks on deck seemed to scream louder. I was privileged to spend one full day a month for an entire year with some of these suffering shepherds in study and in prayer. I saw them cling to each other in some very difficult transitional times, and as one man, cling to the Lord. I heard them weep out their pain when misunderstood and under fire. Many afternoons I saw them on their knees, some of them even facedown on the floor. But God has released enormous blessings to this church through the broken hearts of these shepherds who did their best to listen to the one voice that mattered most. The church is now unified and flourishing after decades of decline.

I think the father of my friend Dee knew this as well and lived it out in spades:

> My father served as a shepherd in a small, mostly white, Southern church during the '70s. Our church of eighty started growing to well over 100. We were bussing in twenty or so African American and lower socio-economic kids. Seven adults also were baptized that year. But war was brewing.
>
> Some didn't want the black children—so they complained about the expense of running a bus. My father pleaded in tears for folks to work together. There was no anger in his voice, but he grieved to see people so hardened against the outcast of the community.
>
> Eventually the elders felt they could not lead those who would not follow, so they resigned and, rather than cause division, dispersed to nearby churches.
>
> Eventually Dad came back. And even though the church no longer officially called him an elder, most saw Dad as a faithful shepherd. And Dad kept serving—even with a broken heart.
>
> Now, years later, he is highly respected in that church which is at peace and flourishing.

Ah, yes! The family of God so needs shepherds with broken hearts.

BROKEN BY SIN

Sometimes a shepherd's heart gets broken by his or her own arrogance and sin. Joe is one of these.

One Sunday morning I saw Kyle, a shepherd, stand before his church to announce a new *part-time* staff person. But the moment Kyle said Joe's name, the church rose in a thunderous shouting and clapping ovation, assuming Joe was to be their *senior minister*. The church never heard the rest of Kyle's announcement; so from that moment on it was virtually impossible for Joe not to be the senior pulpit minister.

That was well over a year ago, but new people are still streaming to that church. Why? Because Joe walked the church through his story. "I am a prodigal returned," Joe had confessed. "I am one who left the joy of my father's house." Here's his story:

In 1967 I enrolled in Bible college. I quickly learned that God had gifted me for preaching. Within two years I was married and off to my first ministerial assignment. Heady stuff for a twenty-year-old!

Doors opened, accolades came. And before long I hit the national speaking circuit. Then larger churches began to call. Some peers called me "the rising young star on the horizon."

The problem was that I believed it. Please understand. I did love Jesus. But looking through the rearview mirror, I can see my "religion" was more about me than about God. In short, here is what happened.

I sank into a cesspool of sin. My sin. My fault. When I finally admitted to myself where I was, I didn't have the strength to free myself. No, I didn't call for help. Where can a popular preacher confess sins without fear of losing his perch?

I trusted no one.

Guilt cascaded over me. Yet I stumbled progressively downward. I began to drink heavily, hiding it from my family and friends—till I was caught and fired.

Not long after, on the fifteenth anniversary of our marriage, I left my wife and moved away. Life seemed over, and I tried to forget about God. I left the joy of my Father's house and spiraled downward into my self-made hell, into the muck of a modern-day pigpen.

I started a new business, but went bankrupt within a year. With no money, no family, no church, and no job, I lived in my car awhile, sometimes going days without eating because I had no money.

I discovered nightclubs. I can't stand to remember everything I did in those days. But one was drugs. I didn't care what. If it stops the pain, you just gulp it down with another shot of vodka. That can kill you.

My second trip to the hospital, the doctor said, "You have only a 50/50 chance of being alive in the morning." I lay there thinking, *I've made such a mess of my life that I'm going to die completely alone.* Torn at first between self-pity and self-loathing, I finally prayed, "God, I'm dying a fool's death. If you can somehow let me live, I promise you, I'll spend the rest of my life learning how to die right."

My life began to change. No, not miraculously. My healing would take a couple more years. But it started there.

I finally experienced the grace and mercy of God. Alice and I remarried just three years after our divorce. We've even had a celebration child since then—fourteen years ago. And I have learned how God heals prodigals like me, who will always be ashamed of what they've done—but who rejoice in the forgiveness of God.[11]

Shepherd Joe has a broken heart. And the morning of the raucous standing ovation, I saw with new eyes how badly we broken sheep need shepherds with broken hearts.

Please understand: I am not suggesting that we can't be good shepherds unless we fall as far as Joe did. But all helpful shepherds must come to a place of brokenheartedness over our own arrogance and sin, if we are to be of any real help to brokenhearted people. God's shepherds stand not *over*, but *among* the sheep, with little to offer each other but our broken hearts and the love of God who keeps on rescuing us and who has "poured out his love into our hearts."[12]

BROKEN BY SUFFERING

Sometimes hearts get broken by suffering, including the kind that comes through violence.

Yesterday Carolyn and I sat in the worship assembly as our son-in-law Randy led Communion. Around us sat several families that have been rescued from the brink and mentored into usefulness, largely through Randy's shepherding. When Randy was asked to be an elder at the young age of thirty-nine, he protested, "I am too young, too immature, with too little wisdom." But the other elders affirmed, "Yes, you are young in years. But not in experience. We have watched you deal with enormous suffering, and the way you have risen above it has made you wise and discerning far beyond your years."

You see, on October 21, 1995, Randy's father was murdered. Shot in his own bedroom by his wife, Randy's stepmother.

This horror triggered multiple waves of anguish for Randy and his family. Besides his own overwhelming grief, Randy saw his two daughters, ages twelve and ten at the time, struggle through enormous shock and overwhelming loss as they processed the bewildering fact that Mar Mar had killed Pa Pa.

The eldest granddaughter stood by the open casket and began to cry, "I am so angry at Mar Mar." The youngest, on the other hand, spotting a news story about some woman convicted of murder and facing the death penalty, burst out, "I don't want to see any more newspapers, ever. I don't want them to do that to Mar Mar."

The whole family went through many months of counseling. Besides, there was the criminal case to deal with. Investigations. Questionings.

Depositions. The trial. Then came the civil case with estate issues. Accusations that Randy was being "vindictive and greedy."

In the end, Mar Mar was found not guilty by reason of insanity.

The yearlong ordeal was the worst of nightmares for Randy. He felt consumed with grief as well as with anger. Night after night he would come home from work, kiss his wife and daughters, then retreat to his study, close the door, and wail out his anguish.

Eventually, Randy moved through the shock and began to see that anger was eating him alive and poisoning his life. Finally, he came to a crucial crossroads: "I must decide whether or not I really believe this 'Jesus stuff.' Because if I really believe it, there is no question what I must do."

Finally, Randy, his wife, Debbie, and their two daughters met with Mar Mar—with a psychologist present to guide the process. Randy said, "Mar Mar, I cannot pretend that you did not kill my father. You did. And you unleashed unspeakable pain on me and on my family. I cannot describe the level of anger I have felt toward you.

God's shepherds stand not *over,* but *among* the sheep.

"But I also want you to know that, in the eyes of Jesus, you are as precious as I am. And I want to honor him and live by his spirit. So today I am making the conscious choice to forgive you. I know that forgiveness is not an event. It is a process. But that process begins here and now and will continue, with God's help."

Randy often says that forgiveness is something like peeling an onion. "You peel away a layer, and it makes you cry. Then you peel another layer, and cry some more. But if you keep peeling and crying, eventually the onion is all gone." Some months after that family meeting, Randy called me to say, "Pappy (that is what my grandchildren call me), the onion seems to be all gone now."

Randy is a brokenhearted shepherd whose very wounds have become his weapons. Remember, as Abraham Heschel says, "The man who has not suffered, what does he know anyway?"

Each Friday morning Randy mentors a dozen men, an ethnic and life-situation mix, mostly new Christians who have two things in common: they all have broken hearts, and they all want to know how to live as fully devoted followers of Jesus.

The Bible tells us that the wounds of the suffering shepherd do indeed become his or her weapons:

> Praise be to the God and Father of our Lord Jesus Christ, the Father of compassion and the God of all comfort, who comforts us in all our troubles, so that we can comfort those in any trouble with the comfort we ourselves have received from God. For just as the sufferings of Christ flow over into our lives, so also through Christ our comfort overflows.[13]

EMBRACE YOUR SUFFERING

No question about it—spiritual leadership does not always make the shepherd feel good. In fact, sometimes it breaks his or her heart. But a shepherd with a broken heart has become much better equipped to care for brokenhearted sheep. In Henri Nouwen's words, that shepherd has become "a wounded healer."

Ah, yes. Embrace your suffering. There is a sense in which being broken is the shepherd's true calling. A broken heart lies at the core of the best of shepherds. Landon Saunders said it this way: "The nails of reality have been driven through the hands and feet of God's man. The sword of the spirit has pierced his side. And out of him flows the very life of God.[14]

CARDIOVASCULAR WORKOUTS
FOR SHEPHERD HEARTS

1. Write down the names of three shepherds you know who have broken hearts.

   a. Pray for them.

   b. As soon as possible, drop a note or call them up and let them know how much you appreciate the way "their wounds have been their weapons."

2. When has your heart been broken? How?

3. Describe, in writing, how this feels.

4. Write out what God has taught (is teaching) you from your "brokenness."

5. Who do you know that is walking around today with a broken heart? How can you be a "tender shepherd" to that person this week?

6. Write down the day and time you will reach out to shepherd that broken heart.

A HEART THAT MOVES AT A MEASURED PACE

"No" is a complete sentence.

Believe me; we do not need hassled, bitter ministers.

We don't want you to talk the talk about this being "the
day the Lord hath made" and that we should rejoice
and savor its beauty and poignancy, when secretly you're
tearing around like a white rabbit: we need you to walk
the walk. And we need you to walk a little more slowly.

—Anne Lamott, to a graduating seminary class

sixteen

A HEART MOVING FROM WARRIOR TO LAMP

Remember your leaders who spoke the word of God to you.
Consider the outcome of their way of life and imitate their faith.

—Hebrews 13:7

Ronald Reagan turned seventy just seventeen days after entering the office of President of the United States. Prior to Reagan, the oldest president to be elected was William Henry Harrison in 1840; he was sixty-eight. Unfortunately, President Harrison caught cold on Inauguration Day and, due to his exhausted condition from the campaign, never recovered. He died one month later. Since then, we as a nation have tended to shy away from older men and have chosen younger men to be our leaders.

This trend holds not just in the presidency, but in nearly all walks of life.

You've been at those retirement parties, right? "Let me introduce George Smith, past president of International Properties." Then George gets a gold watch, a forty-year pin, and a round of applause. *Now* who is he? Nobody, that's who.

When athletes, executives, surgeons, entertainers, farmers—and church leaders—can no longer compete with the energy-intensive, widget-producing pace of the young, they get benched, where at best they may become benign and bored or at worst they become bitter. Twin tragedies result: aging persons get dehumanized on the one hand, and society loses valuable resources on the other.

One day King David was given his gold watch and thirty-year pin and sent home from the action too. The whole thing came about, as it often does, without David's choosing and as a humiliating surprise.

DAVID THE WARRIOR

For years David sat firmly on the throne. His wealth mounted. His power grew. His empire expanded. When another battle broke out on the Philistine front, the old warrior buckled on his scabbard and, as usual, headed for the action. By this time, however, David was more than sixty years of age. He had pretty much run out of gas. The old stamina stalled, and the magnificent reflexes failed.

Spotting David in his exhausted state, an opportunistic cousin of Goliath seized the moment—and would have killed David had not Abishai come to the old man's rescue.[1] How much humiliation can a proud warrior handle in one day? "Thanks, Abishai. I blew that one. Could have taken him easily, but the worn cleats on these old war boots . . . I slipped, Abishai. *Abishai?*"

How could it be? Where is David the warrior? Is this David, son of Jesse, who felled Goliath? Is this the man who brought two hundred Philistine foreskins in a sack and slammed them down on Saul's desk, double dowry for the king's daughter, while the women sang, "Saul has slain his thousands, and David his tens of thousands?"[2] In his prime, David had been no ordinary fighting man. He terrorized the countryside. Around him marched six hundred crack troops, led by thirty mighty men, each with the strength of a hundred men—and *all* had feared David. Is *this* David tired? Does *this* warrior need help in a fight with just one ordinary Philistine?

We feel an awkward silence fall. As David's officers quietly encircle him, gathering the courage for a long overdue confrontation, who spoke first? Abishai? Joab?

"My Lord the King. We . . . we're all your friends, so aside with the formality. David, the time has come for you to hang up your sword. Go home.

Close the book. This chapter of your life is finished. We all swear to you, David; you need to go home. *Now.* For your own good. And for Israel."

The eyes of his officers, first avoiding David's face, now gazed directly at him. This circle of men loved him, but somehow their combined fixed gazes, for the first time in his life, felt intimidating.

David, the time has come for you to hang up your sword. Go home. *Now.*

"But guys, I just slipped. Honest! Go *home?* Ah, yes . . . I guess. Sooner or later. *Now?*"

More silence. The leveled eyes of David's lifetime friends sealed the question.

How does an old warrior feel at such a time? He hesitated and then slowly slid his rusty sword into its sheath for the last time. In resignation, he exhaled a long breath, stumbled toward the chariot, and stiffly dragged himself up. Wheels rumbled on rocks as David's solitary figure sat slouch-shouldered on the chariot that bore him over the horizon toward Jerusalem, sent home from his last battle, dismissed.

Gold watch. Forty-year pin. Golf clubs. David, go home—and stay there!

A glance in the mirror confirmed their advice. No young redheaded warrior stared back from David's looking glass, but an aging man with silver locks and furrowed cheeks. Where great plates of muscle once spanned David's chest, now ribs showed through and loose flab sagged at his middle. The warrior was gone! For good.

DAVID THE LAMP

But wait! Did our old soldier go home to sulk away his later years? Not our David. Already he was dreaming bigger dreams than ever—but quieter, richer, deeper dreams than simply winning wars.

David loved more deeply, enriching his relationships. Most important, David, in his sunset years, grew increasingly alive to God. Yes, he prepared for the temple, bought land, drew plans, and equipped personnel. But he also trained musicians and wrote music for psalms, anticipating the time when praises of Yahweh would ring day and night in the temple courts.

Even more importantly, perhaps, some of David's finest poetry flowed from his pen during his golden, post-warrior days. His wisdom deepened. Perspective enriched his insights. He would write:

The righteous will flourish like a palm tree. . . .
    They will still bear fruit in old age,
        they will stay fresh and green.[3]

Why did this old warrior not "retire" and vegetate after the "useful years of his career" came to a close? What made David different from most millions? The answer lies in the last half of a sentence we interrupted a couple of pages ago. True, David's men did tell him, "Never again will you go out with us to battle," but that was only part of what they said. The last half of their statement explains, "so that the lamp of Israel will not be extinguished."[4] David did not get sent home because he had used up his usefulness. Rather, contrary to the modern view of forced retirement, David's men sent him home *because of* his usefulness. They considered him too valuable as a lamp in Israel to be risked as a warrior in battle. Be careful not to miss this! David saw his own core identity clearly, so he did not pine away in oblivion. He did not define himself by externals as "warrior." While he did soldiering for a certain period of his life, it wasn't who he was. Rather, David saw his real identity as "lamp of Israel." That's who he was.

But he also became a "lamp" for all men, everywhere, for all time. When hearts ache for comfort and eyes long for sight, to what pages have God's people for centuries turned to read? Have they flipped through the battle legends of the "warrior"? No. They have slowly savored the poems and songs radiating from the "lamp of Israel" and carefully reflected on the depths they found there. They still do.

To their great credit, David's men recognized the true heart of the kingdom as a spiritual heart. They valued his spiritual resources over his physical energy. They clearly understood that the hope of Israel lay with the spiritual lamp at its heart, not with the sword swingers at its frontiers. As a result, David mellowed and deepened with age—and all generations of believers since are the better for it!

IN OUR DAY

Our value system in early-twenty-first-century Western culture has gotten turned bottom side up. Progress is productivity. Productivity requires power, so we place our priority on youth, energy, looks, and ambition—a total contrast to David and his men.

For Christians this dehumanizes the aging. Some aging men cling desperately to youthful positions, finally losing their grip and their dignity. Others meekly retire into oblivion.

What is worse, the community of believers loses its lamps. Our adjectives betray us: Dynamic. Aggressive. Energetic. Active. Successful. These words often get used to describe contemporary Christian leaders and churches. Thus, too many would-be spiritual leaders feel they must validate their usefulness by busyness. To stay overcommitted is to look young, energetic—and "useful."

Unfortunately, in our day the Christian community—even those who call themselves "shepherds"—tend to place priority on physical vigor and high-energy "productiveness." We want warriors, not lamps. So when youthful vigor declines, we cast old lamps aside and stumble on in the half-darkness. Triple tragedy results:

First, the elderly are left to sit and wait—for nothing.

Second, the organic body of Christ often becomes distorted until it resembles a corporation.

Third, and most tragic of all, the community of believers attempts to operate on the "arm of flesh," running fast but not deep. It ignores its richest resources: the lamps at the heart of God's people.

All this, despite the fact that, from God's perspective, only age can generate the real soul-curing valuables. Youthful energy produces important things, certainly, but it does not produce the deepest, richest, and most lasting values.

My dear fellow shepherds, we must rediscover the difference between a lamp and a warrior. Real spiritual growth is not geared to productivity, creating careers, and consuming youthful energy. Rather, the church is a family that grows through enriched relationships. The healthy community of faith moves at a measured pace and runs deep. It is not a corporation, but a body with eyes, heart, and soul. The community of faith does not so much need to be jump-started as it needs its darkness illuminated by the lamps of Israel.

It is true that Paul warned Timothy, "Don't let anyone look down on you because you are young."[5] But many aging Christ-followers need someone to remind them, "Don't look down on yourself because you are growing older." Paul also offered young Timothy words of wisdom that could be spoken only from a much older and more experienced person.[6]

Age can be loaded with spiritual resources. Time supplies perspective. David hints toward this: "I was young and now I am old."[7] Years on the road enable us to gather experience, as blind alleys get checked out, temptations are overcome, and skills are learned.

With age, serious believers become our valuable, thoughtful mentors that move at a measured pace. Young believers, tempted to defect, can look up and see ahead of them on the way a gray head that has felt infinitely more pain, discouragement, and temptation than have the young—but that gray head still believes, still travels toward God.

Those of advanced years supply the rich memories that lie at the roots of dreams. This is why Job reminds us, "Is not wisdom found among the aged? Does not long life bring understanding?"[8] Without the lamps of Israel at the heart of the kingdom, warriors on the frontiers may continue to swing their swords awhile, but with diminishing results.

VALUE SPIRITUAL DEPTH

The straight message for younger people is this: be grateful for your energy, but value spiritual depth over high energy. As Russ Blowers says,

> Being old doesn't automatically confer infallibility. It does, however, furnish one with considerable experience in the trenches.
>
> If the elderly upset you by giving unsolicited advice, do not roll your eyes and sigh condescendingly. Listen. You may learn something from some brother or sister who has been there, done that, someone who knows how to navigate the whitewater of shepherding. Timothy was listening to Paul and learning. He knows he won't have Paul around much longer, and he wants to soak up the riches of his advice and teaching.[9]

Seek out the older folks who sparkle, and beat a path to their door. Ask them many questions about the mysteries of life. Listen carefully, not just politely.

Create forms and systems that tap the resources of age rather than sideline it. One retired physician, an elder in our church, resigned from being an "elder," he said, so that he could "do more 'shepherding.'" How ludicrous! This man, and many other spiritual giants like him, retire from church leadership as age advances because they "don't have the energy to attend a hundred meetings a year." What has *that* to do with anything?

Spiritual leadership is about "being" (being a lamp) far more than about "doing" (swinging a sword).

Back before Ed passed away, Ed and Kathryn, a retired couple in our church, spent forty hours per week, for more than fifteen years, running off cassette tapes of messages and classes, labeling and mailing them to the far-flung corners of the globe. They dreaded the rapidly approaching day when "we will no longer have the energy to do this, and we will be so useless."

> Spiritual leadership is about "being" (being a lamp) far more than about "doing" (swinging a sword).

Why should people like Ed and Kathryn, aglow with God-given, mature spiritual insight, not gladly lay down the sword in order to make their soft light available to the younger ones? Enormous value could be gained by couples like these spending those forty (or even just twenty) hours a week simply giving counsel, answering questions, and offering encouragement, as younger strugglers emerge from the ring of darkness just beyond the lamp's pool of warm light.

I dream of a special kind of pleasant park under an atrium, featuring alcoves and chairs and tables. Old and young meet here. At all hours of the day. Older people make themselves available to the younger who come streaming in, exuding energy but needing spiritual resources. As they bask in the light of the aged, the young discuss work, marriage, children. They find wisdom regarding heartache, money, sex. They come asking for resources to confront temptation, loneliness, suffering. The young want to hear seasoned believers talk about death, heaven, doubt. They sense the folly of skipping like speedboats across life's surface and want to learn how to run deep like ocean liners.

Something like this could turn our culture right side up again.

YOUR REAL WORTH

The straight message to the older ones is this: trust what the Word says about your value to those of us who are younger. We need the energy of your spirits in their deep places where the physical energy of our youth is simply inadequate. Your advanced years are too valuable to waste, my friends! Don't cling to youth or mourn lost energy. Go home from the wars, and be something far more important than a warrior.

Be a lamp in Israel.

One of our sons-in-law used to dream of becoming financially independent by age forty so he could spend the rest of his life, self-supported, in full-time ministry. If at forty, then why not at sixty-five? Why not retire to full-time, self-supporting ministry? The fact is, you have no right to withhold your spiritual resources from the family of God. Your family needs you! They feel better with you nearby.

THE GREATER VALUE

In an ancient Taoist legend, a carpenter and his apprentice gazed upon a huge and very old, gnarled oak tree.

The carpenter said to his apprentice, "Do you know why this tree is so big and so old?"

"No," answered the apprentice. "Why?"

"Because it is useless," replied the carpenter. "If it were useful, it would have been cut down, sawed up, and used for beds and tables and chairs. But because it is useless, it has been allowed to grow. And that is why it is now so great that you can rest in its shadow."

Trees are most useful and beautiful as trees, not as furniture.

My friend and brother Earl Kiser died at the age of ninety-eight. At that age he could no longer serve as our church custodian, and he died in a rest home. He had read the Word and walked and talked with God virtually every day of his literate life. I am glad he wasn't sawed and cut into benches, because I needed to sit in his shade. Those last months he could barely shuffle along, but came into the church, pushing that old walker and nodding through my sermons. I felt better with him in the room. I needed him. The fact that he no longer had the energy to clean our church building didn't mean he had lost his value to our church family.

To Earl Kiser and to all those shepherds who have lived quite a long time, longer than some of the rest of us: we need you—desperately.

We need to sit in your shade.

We need you to be our lamps.

Are you approaching what others might call your "sunset years"? Remember: God has a distinct and growing major purpose for you, regardless of your age, and he will provide what you need to meet that purpose. He is looking for shepherds with hearts moving from warrior to lamp!

When you see yourself moving away from your action-intensive warrior years, don't just retire. Rather, transition. Move intentionally into the rich lamp years, and radiate the precious light and gentle power of wisdom and spiritual insight—so desperately needed in our hyperaction-oriented times. Don't retire. Shine! The body of Christ will be the better for it—and so will you!

CARDIOVASCULAR WORKOUTS
FOR SHEPHERD HEARTS

I. Confessions of the chronically overcommitted:

(Circle a Y or N for each of the following statements. Yes, "sounds like me." Or No, "is not me.")

Y   N   I feel driven to help people and serve.

Y   N   In my genuine desire to "serve" and "do right," I sometimes have robbed people of the opportunity to grow and serve.

Y   N   I would rather "over-serve" than have a conflict about someone else "under-serving."

Y   N   I enable others to do less than they could or should, because I will do more and more.

Y   N   I am helping to create unhealthy systems around me (at work, church, family).

Y   N   I want to "fix" things, but I cannot take responsibility for other people's needs, wants, anxiety, or conflicts.

Y   N   When I serve in this way (over-functioning), I send ripples through the system around me.

Y   N   My emotional compass needs to be calibrated by God and the mission he has for me, not by the needs and demands of those around me.

Y   N   I am responsible for this situation; no one else is to blame.

Y   N   I play the central role in keeping this problem in place.

Y   N   I can change only the choices I make.

II. Correctives for the chronically overcommitted: (Questions to ask when choosing work projects)

1. Will this activity be a worthwhile, tangible, and effective way to impact my personal mission?

2. Would this be good or bad for the health of my family relationships?

3. Is this activity likely to result in my over-functioning?

4. Am I able to place enough limits on this project to ensure it does not enable others to under-function?

5. Am I obviously gifted/trained to do this?

6. Can someone else do this project adequately? (Am I really the only one who can do this?)

7. Is there a healthy connection/consistency between this project and other projects I have committed to?

8. Does this energize or drain me?

9. Can I train someone else to do this?

10. Will it take away necessary energy and resources from essential areas of my life?

11. Who is the "client" if I take this on? (the lost, potential leaders, institution, youth, families, church, etc.) Or is there a "shadow client" to deal with?

12. Who can I count on to help me stay accountable to this, to keep me focused on my limits and objectives?

seventeen

A HEART AT PEACE WITH AMBIGUITY

*"My thoughts are not your thoughts, neither
are your ways my ways," declares the LORD.*

—Isaiah 55:8

Aldous Huxley once wrote that human beings are "multiple amphibians"—creatures designed to make our way through many worlds at once: social, spiritual, emotional, cerebral, aesthetic, sexual, psychological, and so on. But, he added, since the industrial revolution harnessed our energies to production and the technological revolution turned us into information manipulators, we tend to live primarily in the two logical worlds of data and productivity. Huxley saw these worlds crowding out our "other worlds," which are thus atrophying. "As a result," he observed, "we are *losing touch with what it means to be human.*"

Rings true for me, Mr. Huxley!

ONE PEG FAITH

Something like what Huxley described can happen to faith, as well. The rational, informational, and linear/sequential worlds of widgets and data tend to dominate in our lives these days. Consequently, the rest of our world suffers neglect, and we are *losing touch with much of what it means to believe.*

The mind-set of the times threatens to strip our faith of symbols, rituals, dramas, mystery, poetry, and story, which say about life and God what logic and reason and rationalism can never say. Instead, we attempt to analyze and explain God. *Scripture* becomes mere religious information and *faith* simply the progressive realization of moral or "religious" goals.

From this perspective we cannot expect anything but flatness. One-dimensional faith, like a tent with only one peg, easily collapses. Yet we Americans tend to secure our faith primarily with the one peg of logical thought. Faith that is only cerebral in content and only behavior-management oriented is one-dimensional.

I am not suggesting that there is something wrong with trying to understand our faith. And certainly nothing is wrong with management of behavior. But many of us attempt to explain the inexplicable, define the indefinable, ponder the imponderable, and "unscrew" the inscrutable. A life of real, meaningful faith can't be treated that way. Trying to do so only leaves people with swollen heads and shrunken hearts.

HAZARDS OF THE QUICK ANSWER

In such an environment, shepherds often find themselves in a conversation that sounds something like this:

Sheep: "I know there is a clear-cut answer; I just don't know what it is. Tell me . . ."

Shepherd: "I cannot answer that question. I am sorry."

Sheep: "What do you mean, you can't answer? You are supposed to be a spiritual leader. What kind of leader are you—I ask and you don't know the answer?"

Those counted on to be spiritual leaders often feel the pressure to explain things. A shepherd's heart must resist that temptation. In fact, quite to the contrary, the heart of a shepherd is a heart of contagious peace even in the absence of closure. This is a heart comfortable with ambiguity, vagueness, "no closure within."

Charisa Hunter-Crump sounds a clear warning against the hazards of quick answers and simplistic thinking:

> Humanity has always gravitated in herds toward the easy answers of conventional wisdom. The easy answers of conventional wisdom play to our conceit, our pride, our desires, our hopes, and our fears. They say life is fair, happiness is earned, prosperity is blessing, God is on our side, evil is out there, truth will be vindicated, and righteousness will be validated. The mystery of God, and the complexity of living, cannot be captured by these easy answers. They seem benign, but they often leave a trail of misery, and eventually confusion, in their wake.
>
> [In shepherding the flock of the eternal and almighty God, we must] not be lulled, cajoled, co-opted, or conscripted by 21st century conventional wisdom—whether political, economic, theological, or cultural. [Sometimes we must even] disturb the calm waters of our easy answers, to reveal the injustices and the uncertainties that lurk beneath, and to live in the chaotic roll and flow of this messy and beautiful life.[1]

DANCING IN MANY WORLDS

God is too vast and mysterious to be confined to linear/sequential thinking and behavior-management activity. That's true of people, as well. There is far more to us than words and mouths and ears and brains. Life is too full of mystery and majesty to be reduced to matters of information and production.

When the Australian aborigine is asked the meanings of mysterious paintings on the wall of a sacred cave, he cannot explain them in words, so he dances his answer! We, too, know very well that many of life's best valuables defy explanation:

- The explanation of love is not love.

- The explanation of a joke is not humor.

- The explanation of music is not music.

- The explanation of a poem is not poetry.

- And the rational explanation of a religious idea or action is not the same as touching the Holy One!

Who can completely diagram the meaning of my wedding ring? Or analyze the meaning of flowers you brought to a hospital room, or explain the bread and the wine of Communion? Sure, you can say words about them that may well be true, but you can never say quite enough, never convey all the truth.

When asked the meaning of one of his stories, Henry Van Dyke replied, "What does it mean? How can I tell you? What does life mean? If the meaning could be put into a sentence, there would be no need of telling the story."[2] And when the great ballerina Anna Pavlova was asked, "Anna, what did you say just now when you danced?" she replied, "If I could tell you, I wouldn't need to dance."

Yes, indeed! When we distance our deeper selves from the fine art of believing, we rob ourselves of most of what it means to believe. Real, dynamic faith takes up our dramatic mysteries and gets inside of them, no matter how undramatic, ordinary, or even misshapen we may think our own lives to be. Full faith gets down to the part of us that we cannot explain or quantify, but that nevertheless shapes the direction of our lives.

So does authentic shepherding! Which means the heart of a shepherd must become at peace with ambiguity and the wonder of the God-man dance.

THE CASE FOR MYSTERY

The Bible doesn't dodge this bullet. In fact, sometimes Scripture seems, at least at first glance, to actually set up unsolvable mysteries, to create impenetrable ambiguities that generate new doubts.

The Bible embraces paradoxes.

For example, the Proverbs say, "Do not answer a fool according to his folly." Then the next verse instructs, "Answer a fool according to his folly."[3] Make up your mind, Solomon! You can't have it both ways. That isn't logical!

Paul charged, "Carry each other's burdens," then added three verses later, "Each one should carry his own load."[4] Who is to bear what burden, apostle?

And again, Scripture declares that Christians are "set . . . free" and should not be "burdened again by a yoke of slavery," yet at the same time we are called to be "slaves to righteousness."[5]

But these are only some of the little paradoxes. There are larger ones, as well: predestination and free will, works and grace, and judgment and mercy, just to mention a few. Possibly you know how to explain these; I must confess that I do not.

And beyond even these are the huge ambiguities of the Bible. If you read long enough, you will be confronted with biblical paradoxes that confound the wisdom of the ages.

The Bible also presents mysteries. For example, God exists. God has all power. God is all knowing. God is all loving. But thousands of people starved to death again this year, and the horror of war has slaughtered thousands more: Why? If God knows, why does he not act? If God loves, why is he not moved to do something? Not enough power? Come on, now. Either God is not all powerful, or he is not all loving, or he is not all knowing, or—he doesn't exist!

I believe the living God not only exists, but knows, loves, and is omnipotent. Yet I do not know how to untangle this dilemma. Oh, I have read great books that address it: C. S. Lewis's *The Problem of Pain* and *God in the Dock*, Philip Yancey's *Disappointment with God*, and others. Yet this mystery still boggles my mind. It has boggled the best minds of the centuries. And the Bible, rather than offering us explanations, compounds these mysteries. For example, what is God up to when Scripture says repeatedly that "an evil spirit from God came forcefully upon Saul"?[6] How can an evil spirit come from God?

HONEY, I SHRUNK GOD

Mystery is precisely the point, isn't it? A God so small that we limited humans can fully explain him is not big enough to be worshiped.

Years back, my friend Juan Monroy, a Christian journalist in Madrid, Spain, was among those who interviewed the American astronaut James Irwin, after Irwin returned from his Apollo 15 mission to the moon. Monroy asked the astronaut, "What did you feel when you stepped out of that capsule and your feet touched the surface of the moon?"

To Monroy's utter surprise, Irwin replied, "Mr. Monroy, it was one of the most profoundly disillusioning moments of my life."

Monroy pressed the astronaut: "How could standing on the moon be so disappointing to a dedicated astronaut like yourself?"

"All of my life," Irwin explained, "I have been enchanted by the romance and the mystery of the moon. I sang love songs under the moon. I read poems by moonstruck poets. I embraced my lover in the moonlight. I looked up in wonder at the lunar sphere and basked in its silver, mysterious glow. But that day when I stepped from the capsule onto the lunar surface and reached down at my feet, I came up with nothing but two handfuls of sterile, gray dirt. I cannot describe the loss I felt as the romance and mystery were stripped away." Then Irwin added, almost plaintively, "Monroy, *there will be no more moon in my sky!*"

Monroy later reflected, "When we come to the place that we think we comprehend and can explain the Almighty, there will be no more God in our heavens."

God's Word not only *reveals* his endless love and awesome holiness, but also *veils* his majesty in mystery and paradox and ambiguity that transcend comprehension. He is God, not human! "'My thoughts are not your thoughts, neither are your ways my ways,' declares the LORD."[7] I think God is also hinting, "And you, my children, are not just mortal, either. You will always be stretching beyond your temporary finitude, watching for glimpses and listening for whispers from infinity."

God has put eternity in our hearts. A part of us lives in worlds beyond, even if we at times find it difficult to stay in touch.

Oh, yes! Because both God and humanity are too big for explanation, the Bible conveys far more than information and logical objectives. In Scripture, God speaks to all of our worlds through drama, music, poetry, stories, paradox, and mystery. The Bible teases out nuances that stretch far beyond mere data in ways too wonderful to explain and too sacred to be contrived. Full faith awakens all of our worlds and dances through them, touching us on multiple levels and moving us with profound force. This kind of faith, like a tent pegged from many angles, is much less likely to go flat.

SHEPHERDING IN THE SHADOW OF MYSTERY

So then, what does all this have to do with having the heart of a shepherd? First and foremost, a shepherd who has stood long before the paradox and mystery of God's majesty and man's complexity will not easily get stampeded into pat answers to profound questions. He or she will offer no simple explanations to inexplicable dilemmas.

A shepherd with a heart at peace with ambiguity and silent before the majesty and mystery of heaven will be of far greater help and comfort than a person who naively attempts to answer every question and explain every mystery. He or she will not feel the compulsion to speak limp and trite words into the place where empathetic silence may be infinitely more appropriate.

I recall one time when my friend David Wray and I felt pressure to answer questions and give comforting explanations. We stood at the door of dear friends whose four-year-old son had just died in his mother's arms on the way to the emergency room. Both David and I felt almost paralyzed by shock and sadness—and in way over our heads. The upturned faces of the distraught parents and their close friends pleaded for explanations, asking for some way to make sense out of this enormous grief. I especially recall David saying, "I would gladly give a hundred dollars a word for the right thing to say in there." But we both knew such words are in short supply, and definitely not for sale. We knew also that words are frail and risky at times like this. Somehow we sensed that silence before such profound grief was so much more helpful than trying to make some kind of sense out of it. Both time and long experience—plus the wonder of the great mysteries—enabled us to resist the strong urge we felt to attempt some words of explanation that might "get the suffering over with" for them.

The flock of God desperately needs shepherds who can stand before the majesty, the mystery, the ambiguity of it all. We must walk at a measured pace with a peace to our steps and a wonder in our souls that also nudges others toward the wonder, and resist the clamor for black and white, pat answers—simple "how to" formulae and empirically measurable results.

AWAKENING YOUR WORLDS

Dear shepherds, let God reawaken all the worlds of your being and ever so gently shape out a rich, full faith with plenty of room for uncertainty—and ambiguity. To do so, however, you may need to make some changes in the way you approach your life.

First, you may need to slow your pace. In our time, so obsessed with speed and productivity, it's always tempting to "grab hold" of faith or to "fix" a broken person in a hurry. In our wild attempts to save time, however, we can easily lose sight of eternity. Faithful living—life full of faith—rarely comes in the midst of hastiness. To find our way into faith, we may need to lower the RPMs and cool our engines. And that is how we can help God-hungry people to do the same.

Second, you may need to still the noise and search for solitude. Learn to listen for God's voice. Elijah listened for God's voice in a mighty wind, in an earthquake, and in a raging fire, but heard him only in a

We must walk at a measured pace with a peace to our steps and a wonder in our souls.

"still small voice."[8] In a world saturated with woofers, tweeters, traffic, television, jet whistles, disk jockeys, rock bands, sirens, and screams, how does a person contemplate the God of the still, small voice?

The psalmist says, "Be still, and know that I am God."[9] Henri Nouwen cautioned, "The word is the instrument of the present world, and silence is the mystery of the future world." Silence may be difficult to find in our world, but nurturing deep roots of faith demands that we search for silence till we find it.

To explore our own doubt and faith and to confront the Holy One, we absolutely must escape the superficial chatter of continuous social interactions and activities and find large chunks of solitude, even in the midst of hectic and overpopulated days.

Third, to awaken all your worlds, you may also need to simplify and prioritize the intake of your life. We get to life just as the Bible says, through the narrow gate. No one reaches a full life via the broad way, which seeks to accumulate as many things, ideas, and experiences as possible. Too much will smother us.

Novelist Thomas Wolfe, eager for full life, once said that he wanted "to ride in all the trains, read all the books, and sleep in all the beds." I can understand Wolfe's feelings. I, too, am incurably curious and tend to draw myself into constant overcommitment lest I "miss something."

But a helpful shepherd of God's people keeps learning that at this pace he does not exhaust events; they exhaust him. Vitality consists in quality of life, not merely in quantity. Yes, in one sense, eternal life is life that lasts forever. But that is nowhere near the whole story. An eternity of low-quality life would be a curse, not a blessing.

Actually, the biblical concept of eternal life, when Scripture is taken all together, has much more to do with how well we live than it does with how long! Perhaps this is why Francis of Assisi advised:

If you want to live life free,
> Take your time, go slowly,
Do few things, but do them well,
> Heart-felt joys are Holy.

Fourth, to keep in touch with all that you are and all that God is, you may need to become more reflective. Scripture reminds us that the really blessed people meditate day and night on their Lord and so are like trees planted by the river, drinking up nourishment and life. Rich faith doesn't stop at the surface level. It is planted in fertile soil and draws life from the deep places. The psalmist goes on to indicate that those who don't dig in and go deep get pushed around a lot. They are at the mercy of their environment, like the "chaff that the wind blows away."[10]

Authentically God-hungry people look for shepherds that will help them run deeper into the heart of God. And the deepest meaning and vitality is found in the mystery of things, even the smallest and most commonplace.

seventeen: A HEART AT PEACE WITH AMBIGUITY

"We need eyes that see and ears that hear . . . because down under the surface, beneath what we have always seen and heard and always expect to see and hear, run deeper meanings and realities waiting to be tapped," says Samuel Miller. "We need to cast away our precious securities, in order to see what is happening for the first time at a new level, with all the fresh vigor of creation's first morning. . . . Creation is still a reality, but only when we are able and willing to stand face-to-face with its disturbing mystery. It is a mystery that constitutes the climate for believing and without the mystery any faith is a bore."[11] And I would add that without mystery, any shepherding is superficial at best and terribly misleading at worst.

DARE TO DIVE IN

Dare to reflect! Settle down beside the drama, the poetry, the mystery of whatever faith you have. Reflect on the tough stuff too: pain, boredom, disappointment, sickness, tragedy, death, life, birth, and nature. This will wake up your slumbering self at levels that can be reached in no other way. Don't be afraid to do this! The Christian faith looks further into what life means than most casual observers see at first glance.

Don't merely analyze faith. Revel in it. In *him*! He won't let you drown. And your task as a shepherd is to help people learn how to swim. It is not merely to explain that the chemical composition of water is H_2O.

Sure, this may require new habits of thought, new disciplines, and new direction. The miracle, however, is not your own ability to be reborn, but the unlimited grace available to you. This also gives you the calmness to be a non-anxious presence in the face of anxiety, panic, chaos, and conflict.

The very ambiguity and mystery can shape your heart into the heart of a shepherd. And shape you into the kind of person God-hungry people want to be like.

CARDIOVASCULAR WORKOUTS
FOR SHEPHERD HEARTS

1. Describe the last time you felt pressured to give a superficial answer for a very complex situation.

2. What mysteries confound you most?

3. List three steps you can take to "awaken your other worlds."

4. Write down a date and place you will take the first step.

eighteen

A HEART THAT DOESN'T WRING ITS HANDS

A "non-anxious presence" is a person who can be present and non-anxious in the midst of others' anxiety.

—Rabbi Edwin Friedman

A friend from the South writes, "An elder called not long ago to voice concern about the flock under his care. 'If I'm a rock, then I've been reduced to the size of a pebble,' he said. 'I haven't had a good night's sleep in three months. I snap at my wife. I've lost all joy in worship.' In fact, he dreaded attending the worship assemblies, lest he get cornered by some irate member. He continued, 'I feel caught in the middle of not just two, but four or five factions in my church. It's not just worship wars, leadership, relevance, role of women—but all of these, intensely, at the same time. I don't know how it got this way. Six months ago we were doing better than we ever had, but recently the place has started unraveling. I don't know what to do, and I'm not sure I can take it any more.'"

Most shepherds have felt such moments of high anxiety, at least now and then. And church trouble seems to show no signs of letting up. In fact, churches may be more vulnerable to tension and anxiety than most institutions. Secular organizations can afford to come down hard on factions that act out, whereas churches want to be kind and tolerant. Consequently, as John Eldredge points out, "There are pastors and Christian leaders who hide behind the fig leaf of 'niceness' and 'spirituality' and never, ever confront a difficult situation."[1] So leaders more easily "neglect discipline, avoid conflict, and abide almost anything to keep people happy."[2]

Then, of course, some church leaders are the extreme opposite, overreacting at the slightest tensions. For example, a minister called this morning seeking advice on how to deal with an elder who explodes into loud, controlling outbursts of rage at the slightest provocation.

Carlus Gupton points out, "Anxious, conflicted churches tend to politicize leaders, treating them as elected representatives and pressuring them to rashly champion the agenda of this or that faction. They also demand quick solutions without allowing the time for adequate deliberation. They push leaders to be reactive and rash. But if a leader is free to shepherd from a peaceful spiritual center, he or she will not easily be politicized, polarized, or threatened." This anxiety often shows up in flurries of hurried and tense meetings, followed by public statements read from the pulpit, poorly thought-out. Which, in turn, spreads the anxieties through the whole church.

All churches, whether troubled or not, need calm, non-anxious leaders who differentiate themselves from the heat of the conflict and focus on the best long-range courses of action. Scripture says that a shepherd must be balanced; or better said, "Temperate, self-controlled, respectable . . . not violent but gentle, not quarrelsome."[3]

James underscores this need for balance and levelheadedness:

If any of you lacks wisdom, he should ask God, who gives generously to all without finding fault, and it will be given to him. But when he asks, he must believe and not doubt, because he who doubts is like a wave of the sea, blown and tossed by the wind. That man should not think he will receive anything from the Lord; he is a double-minded man, unstable in all he does.[4]

MODELED BY A SOOTHING SAVIOR

Perhaps James is calling for what he had seen in Jesus. A storm blew up on the sea, the disciples panicked, but Jesus slept soundly in the back of the boat. When they woke him in fear, he chided them: "O ye of little faith."[5]

By contrast, a heart that does not wring its hands is full of big faith. In the time of confusion and stormy emotion, this heart will say, "We know God is faithful. Let's just stay calm." A shepherd with this kind of heart doesn't wring his hands or overreact. Doesn't get infected with the anxiousness around him or her and jerkily react. This shepherd knows a calming Power much larger than the raging waves. A temperate, balanced shepherd can guide his or her sheep through the storm, because he doesn't take his eyes off of Jesus.

NON-ANXIOUS PRESENCE

Rabbi Edwin Friedman speaks of this demeanor as a "non-anxious presence."[6] By this he means an individual with the ability to be very present in the midst of others' anxiety, remaining connected to the people, and yet at the same time remaining non-anxious. For Friedman, the non-anxious person takes maximum responsibility for his or her own destiny and emotional well-being, and thus provides the maturity to lead others away from their paralyzing or chaotic, hand-wringing anxiety.

Art was a mature and experienced shepherd in our Texas church when a young man with a great heart but little "combat experience" joined our circle of elders. I shall never forget an exchange between these two men. The elders and staff and spouses of our church were on a chartered bus headed to visit the leaders of a sister congregation that partnered with us on some mission projects. Art sat almost asleep, with his Stetson tipped down over his eyes and his long legs sprawled in the aisle. The young shepherd rose from his place and perched on the arm of the seat across from Art, literally wringing his hands, every line of his body language screaming anxiety.

"Art," he spoke rapidly, his voice tense, "we have a major crisis about to break loose in the church."

"Tell me about it," Art calmly responded, slowly shifting his hat to the back of his head, giving full eye contact to the anxious young shepherd.

"Well, some troubled people have come to me, very upset. *They* are going to make big problems. Why, did you know *they* said that . . . ? And *they* are talking to . . . ?"

The younger man worried on awhile. Art listened, not moving.

Finally, Art drawled, "Oh yes, son. I know who *they* are. *They* usually sit near the north wall of the auditorium, about seven rows back. *They* have gone through cycles of this for decades. But nobody takes their complaints seriously. What *they* really need is just a bit of love and attention. They have lots of pain in their world. So every few months I take *them* to lunch, listen to 'em a bit, and love on 'em a lot. And they are OK for a while. Naw, Son, don't you worry about *them*. It's gonna be all right."

> Ever composed, Jesus *responded* rather than *reacted* as the "leaders" had hoped he might.

Then, non-anxious Art pulled his Stetson back down over his eyes and slid back into his nap. I think Art learned this spirit from Jesus. Whenever memory takes me again to that moment, somehow I see Jesus, asleep in the back of a boat.

Jesus consistently modeled a "non-anxious presence," whether asleep among angry waves or awake among angry people. Like the time religious power brokers brought him a woman caught in adultery. Trying to trap Jesus, they said, "Moses commanded us to stone such women. Now what do you say?" Jesus calmly and wordlessly knelt and scribbled in the dirt, then stood and said, "If any one of you is without sin, let him be the first to throw a stone at her." Eventually each man left. Jesus then quietly urged the woman to abandon her sin. Jesus modeled a non-anxious presence. He refused to get caught up in the issue. Ever composed, Jesus *responded* rather than *reacted* as the "leaders" had hoped he might.[7]

Jon Mullican, a student of healthy church systems, says, "To be both engaged and yet calm in the midst of others' anxiety is a significant sign of maturity." Jon believes that when anxiety spikes, people tend to either freeze, flee, or fight.

Some people freeze into indecisiveness. When they do, the shepherd with "a heart that does not wring its hands" remains creative and flexible, considering options.

Others flee from the problem, in panic. When they do, the mature one stands non-anxiously in his place, ready to face the problem.

And some people fight. When these react and brawl, the temperate, balanced, mature shepherd responds calmly, gently, but with firm resolve.

In 1846 Abraham Lincoln ran for Congress against an evangelical Methodist, Peter Cartwright. During the campaign, Lincoln attended a religious gathering. Cartwright gave a stirring address, after which he invited all those who wished to go to heaven to stand up. A few rose to their feet. "Now all those who do not wish to go to hell will stand." The entire audience stood up, with the exception of Mr. Lincoln.

Seeing an opportunity to embarrass his foe, Cartwright asked Lincoln before the entire audience, "Where are you going?"

Lincoln stood up calmly, "I came here as a respectful listener. I did not know that I was going to be singled out by brother Cartwright. I believe in treating religious matters with due solemnity. I did not feel called upon to answer as the rest did. Brother Cartwright asked me sincerely where I was going. I desire to reply with equal directness. I'm going to Congress."[8]

Lincoln did not freeze, flee, or fight. He remained non-anxious in a tense situation and at the same time remained connected to people, even his adversaries. He not only rose above the anxiety, he even diffused it with a word of humor.

NON-ANXIOUS NEHEMIAH

Jon Mullican further reminds us that Nehemiah was a "non-anxious presence":

> Nehemiah returned to the ruins of Jerusalem to restore the city. He rallied the remnant people of Israel, and they immediately began rebuilding the wall. Several naysayers and antagonistic groups attempted to intimidate the workers and stall the work. Then word came to Nehemiah and his workers that the enemies were about to attack. Listen to the anxious voices around Nehemiah:
>
> We are exhausted: "The strength of the laborers is giving out, and there is so much rubble that we cannot rebuild the wall."
>
> We are doomed: "Our enemies said, 'Before they know it or see us, we will be right there among them and will kill them and put an end to the work.'"
>
> We are outnumbered: "Then the Jews who lived near them came and told us ten times over, 'Wherever you turn, they will attack us.'"
>
> The situation became highly charged with anxiety: Nehemiah's workers were anxious. The antagonists also became anxious, fearing the Jews might actually succeed in rebuilding the wall and take power.
>
> However, rather than joining in the anxious fray of his people and of their enemies, Nehemiah remained calm, creative, and

204

focused on the goal. He calmed his people's fears and then galvanized them to action. In fifty-two days the wall stood at its full height. Rather than freeze, flee, or even fight, Nehemiah led his people through the emotional pain to which they subjected themselves and accomplished the task.[9]

KNOW YOURSELF

One major part of a non-anxious presence is the capacity to self-differentiate. What a big word: *self-differentiation*. Put simply, it means "to define ourselves and our own life goals apart from surrounding group pressures." To be self-differentiated is to be who we are in the presence of anxious others, while still remaining connected to those who feel uptight. Murray Bowen described the ability to know who we are apart from others as "differentiation of self." Differentiation of self might include:

- The ability to steer one's own course in the turbulent waters of a living system.

- The ability to allow the life and teaching of Jesus to serve as one's compass, rather than reading everyone else's emotional chart.

- Being a less-anxious presence in the midst of others' anxieties.

- The ability to take responsibility for one's own emotions and feelings, rather than expecting others to deal with them.

- The ability to know the difference between thinking and feeling.

A leader with the capacity to know and do the right thing understands himself or herself apart from the others and so is able to achieve distance from a situation and observe what is really going on, without letting personal reactivity or anxiety get in the way.[10]

Jesus knew who he was and clearly understood his purpose. So he moved at a measured pace. In his own time he let the violent crowd know who He was and where He stood; but he did not disconnect his heart from these people nor from his values. He valued the law. He valued the women. He valued even those who tried to trap him.

These vignettes—asleep among the waves and on his knees among hostile people—give just two glimpses into what Jesus does consistently.

When I took the pulpit of a fairly high-profile Texas church, a former minister gave me some good advice. "The visibility of this church will make you a public figure," he warned, "and people from all over will want a piece of you. Most won't understand the crucible you live in. Even ministers of other large churches won't. Some of your friends will feel hurt because you cannot do for them what they once expected. This will tear you apart. So you will have to draw some boundaries."

How right he was. I have always found it hard to set boundaries. So I tried to please everybody, and wound up constantly overcommitted, excelling at little, and pleasing almost nobody. I could feel anxiety rising.

To be a non-anxious presence, I had to get a healthier sense of my own person and clarify my motives. I discovered that at least part of my rising anxiety came from my need for approval and acceptance. So to avoid being a hand-wringing anxious presence, I had to come to terms with this insecurity.

I also learned that I must have a clearer sense of my own calling and mission. I had to differentiate myself from the role that people expected me to play and instead decide:

1. what I do *best*. Then,

2. what *matters most*. Then,

3. what must be *done first*.

This process helped me to see that I was not (and am not) able to take every appointment nor return every phone call or e-mail. Since even closest friends did not always understand this, it was (and is) painful. This means I have to continually clarify my self-understanding and personhood. I have to continually "self-differentiate."

You must, too.[11]

MODEL PEACE

We cannot run from people in order to remain non-anxious. Nor can we duck anxious situations. On the contrary, a good shepherd will differentiate himself or herself from the problem, yet remain deeply connected to the people.

Carlus Gupton observes, "In anxious times, shepherds who 'do not wring their hands' avoid two extremes. 'Quick fixes' on the one hand. And superficial religiosity which disdains thoughtful intervention on the other hand. Between these two extremes is a kind a soulful engagement."

The apostle Paul modeled such "soul-full engagement" as he refereed an anxious tension in the church at Philippi, apparently triggered by a squabble between two prominent women.[12] First, *the apostle modeled a non-anxious presence*:

> Whatever you have learned or received or heard from me, or seen in me—*put it into practice*. And the God of peace will be with you.[13]

In a conflicted, anxious church of our day, a calm shepherd can still "put into practice" by modeling peace. Anxious, harried, irritable leaders cannot shepherd at their best.

Second, *Paul prayed and urged these women to pray as well*. Without God's peace, a shepherd may be inclined to wring his or her hands and spread even more anxiety and chaos. But prayer changes things:

> In everything, by prayer and petition, with thanksgiving, present your requests to God.

And then he promises that "the peace of God, which transcends all understanding"[14] will flow out of intimate communion with the peace-giving God.

Third, while handwringers seem to expect the worst from people, *Paul urges us to expect the best.* Listen for the bright note in his voice:

> Finally, brothers, whatever is true, whatever is noble,
>> whatever is right, whatever is pure, whatever is lovely,
>>> whatever is admirable—if anything is excellent
>>>> or praiseworthy—think about such things.[15]

Here Paul was not telling Christians to ponder warm and fuzzy devotional notions (though there is clearly an important place for that). Rather, he urges them—and us—to ponder the best attributes in the very people *with whom we have had issues*, rather than dwell on their failures and faults.

THE BEST LEADERSHIP

At the end of the day, the best leadership emerges from hearts that do not wring their hands in human anxiety but remain firmly rooted in God's presence and power. Jon Mullican tells the story of two non-anxious shepherds with whom he has had the pleasure of serving God:

> Ken and Jack are wise and insightful shepherds. Beginning in 1969, Marvin, the first minister of our church in Tulsa, led her to become a dynamic and trailblazing congregation. After twenty-seven years of service, Marvin transitioned to a "ministry at large" of writing and lecturing.
>
> The following seven years became tumultuous times. Several groups became upset, and some left the church. Ministers misbehaved. Congregants anxiously demanded drastic action. Along with low morale, economic downturns resulted in short funds. Plus many more crises.

However, through it all, Ken and Jack continued to calm nerves and to maintain serenity in their own lives—even through illness and death in their own families. No matter the circumstances, Ken and Jack remained ever upbeat, always seeking options, never hand-wringing. Their calm became contagious among other key leaders as well—and then spread across the church. This allowed the church to negotiate the transition from Marvin's banner years, through the turbulent times, to the relative calm that followed.

Oh yes, in our turbulent times and tumultuous lives, we desperately need the calming presence of shepherds that do not wring their hands. Look away from this page a moment, and examine your hands. Those hands are the extension of your heart. What do you want them to be doing when the pressure of crisis mounts? God wants to use your hands and your heart as a calming presence in the midst of the storm.

CARDIOVASCULAR WORKOUTS
FOR SHEPHERD HEARTS

To be both engaged and yet calm in the midst of others' anxiety is a significant sign of maturity. *What about you?*

Get a pad and pen, and write out specific actions you might take in your congregational or family setting that would apply each of the following principles from Nehemiah and Paul:

NEHEMIAH:

1. When anxious people freeze into indecisiveness, how would you remain creative and flexible and calmly consider options?

2. When anxious people flee from the problem in panic, how would you stand non-anxiously in your place, ready to face the problem?

3. When anxious people fight, how would you respond with firm resolve?

PAUL:

1. How would you refuse to become hooked into the dysfunction of others by anxious reactivity?

2. How would you redirect anxieties into prayer and thanksgiving, to be at peace in God's control?

3. How would you refocus attention on the best attributes of those with whom you differ?

ADDITIONAL QUESTIONS FOR REFLECTION:

1. To what degree does the anxiety of another upset me?

2. How free do I feel to express my own thinking, to set my own boundaries?

3. How much do I depend on another's calmness or happiness to make me calm or happy?

4. How well am I able to stay connected to people and take a position when the emotional atmosphere gets intense?

5. How well am I able to see my own part in a chronic pattern in my family, church, or workplace—and then alter it?

6. To what degree am I able to be neutral, refuse to blame or diagnose others, and refuse to take others' reactions and behavior personally?

7. How well do I take responsibility for my own emotions rather than for the emotions of others?

8. How well am I able to express my own beliefs without demanding that others accept them? (Allowing others to disagree with my convictions without feeling they have rejected me[16]

A HEART
FLOODED
WITH HOPE

The future is as bright as the promises of God.

—M. Norvel Young

nineteen

A HEART OF ENCOURAGEMENT

He was glad and encouraged them all to remain true to the Lord with all their hearts. He was a good man, full of the Holy Spirit and faith, and a great number of people were brought to the Lord.

—Acts 11:23–24

He was just a little boy when the pivotal moment came. But as a grown man, he is still shaped by those few brief words of encouragement.

"When I was nine years old, my parents joined a new and small congregation in south Dallas. There were not many children there, especially boys my age. In fact, the Wednesday night Bible class I attended consisted of six girls and me. In our type of church, back then, that meant I led every prayer."

This nine-year-old was a bashful little fellow to begin with, and now totally outnumbered by girls, the circumstances began to wear on him. One day he found himself all alone in a Sunday-school room, feeling sidelined and sad.

"I was allowing myself a pretty big pity party, wishing I was somewhere else," he recalls. "That's when 'Brother Ware' walked in. He was one of our elders, and I knew he was a much-respected man in our church. 'Brother Ware' managed to squeeze his body into one of the little desks across from mine and said, 'Ricky, I understand from your parents that you want to be a preacher when you grow up.'

"'Yes, sir, Brother Ware,' I replied. 'I do.'

"Then he put his hand on my back and said, 'Well, I think you will become a great preacher, and I'm so glad you're growing up in this church. I'm proud of you.'"

That little boy, now a grown man by the name of Rick Atchley, has indeed become a great preacher. He is known to hundreds of thousands of people as a man of God. Rick stands before some 4,000 people every Sunday in his home church in North Richland Hills, Texas. His books and audio recordings circulate to legions beyond those walls, and God is using Rick as one of the significant shapers of an entire movement.

But Rick still remembers that brief touch of a hand and those loving words of encouragement as a key moment in his spiritual formation. In fact, Rick says, "I tell people that was my ordination. It was almost forty years ago, and I still have vivid memories of the moment. It was the first time anyone ever told me that I could be a difference-maker for God and his kingdom. I don't ever remember feeling sorry for myself again."

Rick adds this postscript: "By the way, when I first told the story, I talked about this big man who showed me such kindness. But not long ago his grandson, Phil Ware, told me his grandpa was actually a small man, probably only about five foot six. Maybe he just seemed big because I was so young. Then again, in his own way, 'Brother Ware' was a giant to me."

Oh, yes! The heart of a shepherd must never underestimate the incredible life-shaping power of even the smallest word of encouragement, spoken by a shepherd to one of his lambs who loves and respects him or her.

SON OF ENCOURAGEMENT

Question: Besides Jesus, who would you name as the key player in the early church? Paul, maybe? Or Peter? Both are towering figures, to be sure. Yet I would vote for a man named Joseph (or Joses). You may not recognize him by that name. But you would know him by his nickname: *Barnabas*, the "Son of Encouragement."[1]

I give Barnabas top billing because his heart of encouragement saved the day at several pivotal points during the formative years of the faith.

First, right after Pentecost, hundreds of new Christians had run out of money in Jerusalem and were headed home to distant towns, without yet being fully grounded in the faith. But Barnabas led the way, it seems, and hundreds pooled their resources to support the new Christians until they got better grounded.[2]

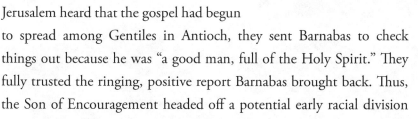

The heart of a shepherd must never underestimate the incredible life-shaping power of even the smallest word of encouragement.

Second, after Paul met Christ on the Damascus road, he returned to Jerusalem. The Jerusalem folk feared Paul's intentions, however, since the last time they saw him he had been killing Christians. But Barnabas became Paul's credibility witness to the Jerusalem church, thus saving the faith and later the ministry of this new disciple.[3]

Third, when Jewish Christians in Jerusalem heard that the gospel had begun to spread among Gentiles in Antioch, they sent Barnabas to check things out because he was "a good man, full of the Holy Spirit." They fully trusted the ringing, positive report Barnabas brought back. Thus, the Son of Encouragement headed off a potential early racial division in the church.[4]

Fourth, when the Antioch church needed a leader, Barnabas "found Paul." He had been keeping up with Paul and was a good judge of character, so Barnabas introduced Paul to the leadership of the Antioch church. In this way Barnabas not only preserved unity between Jewish and Gentile churches in those formative years, but he also encouraged the Antioch church on to the next level by providing them with an outstanding leader. He also launched the ministry of young Paul—who later became the world-changer we know today.[5]

Fifth, when Paul and Barnabas later became partners in missionary work, they fell into a sharp disagreement over John Mark. The young man had wimped out on the first mission trip, so Paul would not let him go on the second. While Paul went on with the mission, Barnabas accompanied John Mark back to the young man's hometown. And apparently Barnabas, the Son of Encouragement, then mentored John Mark to usefulness; later Paul sent for John Mark because he thought the young man would be "helpful to me in my ministry."[6] In other words, "John Mark has been mentored by Barnabas, so he will be a good one."

Barnabas, Son of Encouragement, encouraged the dispersing new Christians in Jerusalem to mature. He encouraged the Jewish church to accept Paul, thus giving Paul a good start. He encouraged the spread of the gospel in Antioch and encouraged unity between the Antioch and Jerusalem churches. He encouraged the growth of the Antioch church, giving them a leader, and at the same time encouraged the launch of Paul's ministry. He encouraged Paul in his mission work. And he encouraged John Mark, who not only joined Paul, but had a great ministry of his own, even writing one of the Gospels, according to tradition. Barnabas was a strategic and consistent encourager.

Like all great shepherds, Barnabas had *a heart of encouragement.*

A BARNABAS ON YOUR BLOCK

Barnabas, we need you now. Today's Christ-followers still need wave after wave of authentic encouragement, especially from Christian leaders. Brother Ware "strategically encouraged" Rick Atchley, and now hundreds of thousands reap the harvest sown in that brief, godly encounter in a small classroom between one man and one boy.

Fortunately, many modern-day Barnabases are walking quietly through many communities of faith, even today.

Ellis Krogsgaard crossed my path when he coached my high-school hockey team, more than fifty years ago. "Ellie" was an encourager even then. In the decades since, every encounter with this man I love ever so much has lifted my spirits and left me with a warm glow flooding my heart. He is also a lamp at the heart of the church where he has long served as an elder.

His wife struggled with ill health for many years. Ellie himself has battled a pronounced physical disability most of his life and more recently has been fighting cancer. Yet he remains constantly upbeat. His positive outlook is contagious. Because of his unique way of making people feel significant, he connects with all ages. And Ellie embodies the adage, "If you can't say something good, say nothing."

Just a few weeks ago, at my fiftieth high-school reunion, I saw Ellie again. Sunday morning I watched him close his eyes and raise his hands in worship. I witnessed his love for God's Word, riveted—as usual—on the message. Then I got to be in front of him. In those few brief moments, he gave me a huge bear hug and spoke words of affirmation into my heart. Those brief moments have energized me with weeks of lifted spirits.

Coach Ellie is definitely a shepherd with a heart of encouragement.[7]

My friend Lou sees a heart of encouragement in Randy Becton. Though Randy battled cancer and the aftermath of many rounds of chemotherapy, for decades he served as a gentle shepherd among the elders of a church where Lou and I served as soul brothers. "While cleaning up my files," Lou writes, "I found literally hundreds of messages of encouragement and appreciation from Randy. He even enclosed a $100 bill in one of them!"[8]

A colleague, Dean Owen, himself a shepherd, remembers two mentors with hearts of encouragement:

I've known John and Jewell Barnett (parents of widely-known minister Joe Barnett) since I was about six years old. John was a shepherd at our church, then he moved with the younger couples when our church planted a daughter church. My parents were one of these "younger couples." I was ten at the time, but still remember walking down the hallway toward the auditorium after Bible class. A strong hand clasped my shoulder, and John would call my name, turn me around, and ask about me or tell something he admired about me. This happened almost weekly until I left for college seven years later.

That he even knew my name amazed me, but when he would mention specific things he admired in me, it just blew me away. Those encouraging words came when I hardly believed in myself. For him to say them to me was too good to be true. Through life I've been blessed by encouraging words from many people, but none have impacted me like those early words from John.

Before we left the old church, Jewell mentored my mom and John mentored my dad to teach the junior-high boys and girls. For years after John and Jewell retired from teaching, my mom and dad continued to shape the lives of young people as John and Jewell had mentored them. Later Dad also became a shepherd, and my parents formed a team like John and Jewell.

John always assumes the best about people, and they usually live up to his expectations. I don't get to see them very often anymore, but to this day, if I just catch sight of them, my heart leaps. Now I'm a shepherd myself, and I carry around in my heart a picture of the kind of shepherd I want to be. That picture has John Barnett's face on it.

Even a small gesture of encouragement can go a long way. For example, Carolyn recently sent a small, decorative bird's nest of brightly colored artificial eggs to a "weary Tennessee shepherd." She received the following reply:

> God knew I couldn't take another gray day, so he used you to send me a breath of spring. I love the bird nest; it is sitting on my mantel, and each time I pass through that room, I know spring is Eternal and that Carolyn Anderson loves me. I love you to the moon and back,
>
> Rose

STEP INTO THE PICTURE

One encouraging heart can ignite a flame in thousands. An Olympic flashback takes us back to 1988 in Seoul, South Korea. The event I have in mind did not appear on TV, but it inflames my heart still today.

Arlene Lima, a twenty-two-year-old Chicagoan and a senior pre-law student at DePaul University, competed in an experimental sport, Tai Kwon Do. Arlene scored an upset in the women's welterweight division, winning the gold. She stood on the medal podium, waiting for the national anthem to begin. All went quiet—too quiet. The tape had broken! Although Arlene was a rather bashful person, when the silence seemed to grow unbearable, she began to sing softly, "Oh say can you see . . ."

Then her parents joined in. Soon a large contingent of GIs joined the song, as well. The anthem swelled louder and louder as even more Americans raised it louder still, till the whole crowd got up, tears streaming down their faces, following with gusto the waving arms of the impromptu athlete-become-conductor of this grand choir.

People said it was the most moving awards ceremony of the '88 games. A formality had been transformed into a never-to-be-forgotten event. One girl's unsteady voice provided the overture for an impromptu chorus *that moved a world!*

Things like this happen more often than you think. Tremendous power lies in one act of encouragement!

Be the one person whose heart of encouragement at God's strategic moment can make the big difference.

One teenager stands up and says, "I don't care what the rest of you are going to do; I'm not going to do drugs or play with sex. I want to serve people, not use them." Then a whole chorus of others say, "Me too."

One family on the block notices a minority couple that has moved in. "We'll be the first to have them in our home," they say. Next thing you know, everybody on the street invites them over.

One man stands up in a meeting and says, "We are going to run this company to build people, not just make money." And a chorus of others joins in and says, "That is just what I wanted somebody to say."

One courageous preacher stands up and says, "I am tired of climbing the ladder. Instead of looking for a bigger church or a more visible role in the church, I want to shepherd right here. But I'm no longer content with 'religion as usual.'"

Never, ever, underestimate the influence of one totally authentic servant life. The world changes person by person. Block by block. Precinct by precinct. City by city. Nation by nation. Indeed, the whole world can be changed soul upon soul, like a forest fire spreading from one flaming tree to the next—until the mountains are set ablaze.

And the most strategic people to kindle the fire are spiritual leaders with hearts to encourage the flock, one sheep at a time. Why not be one of them?

CARDIOVASCULAR WORKOUTS
FOR SHEPHERD HEARTS

For several years a friend and former minister periodically took me to lunch and said, "This is my Encourage Lynn Anderson Day." I shall never forget how much those lunches meant. You likely remember similar experiences.

First, write down the names of people who encouraged you at strategic moments. Then:

a. Call or write and thank them for that encouragement. (If they are deceased, write them anyway! It will grow your own heart.)

b. Tell several other people the story of those moments of encouragement.

Second, write down the names of people to whom you could speak a word of encouragement. (Some may feel deeply discouraged, while others may be doing well, but they might be lifted to new heights by a strategic word of encouragement).

Third, write down a specific day that you will encourage them, either by letter or phone call or conversation.

I criticize by creating something beautiful.

—Michelangelo

twenty

A HEART THAT EXPECTS GOOD THINGS AHEAD

The most pathetic person in the world is someone
who has sight, but has no vision.
—Helen Keller

One evening Carolyn and I flipped on CNN and found Larry King interviewing First Lady Laura Bush. King lobbed her an open-ended question about how the first family had coped with the monumental stresses after 9/11. Mrs. Bush calmly replied, "Well, Larry. We have a strong faith, you know." King's body language shifted, and his voice gathered intensity: "But our world is getting worse, not better. So my real question is: In the midst of today's global polarization, carnage, and hopelessness, how can you hang on to your faith?"

How indeed? *I really, really* needed to hear her answer. In the face of a world gone mad, I found myself struggling to hold on to my own faith!

GLOBAL CHAOS

A few days before this interview, the *New York Times Weekend* magazine had carried a story from Afghanistan. My son Christopher, a photojournalist, and his friend Mike Finkel chronicled their conversation with Naji, a young Taliban fighter who had gone AWOL and fled north.

Naji was sick of war and deeply disillusioned with the Taliban. But his only education consisted of rote religious memorization. He had no job skills beyond fighting. And, Naji explained, all his friends faced the same blank wall.

"No war, no way to make a living, and I don't know anyone different from me," he said. Now multiply Naji's plight by the millions of young men in Afghanistan. Multiply that number again by the number of countries in the Middle East and Africa. Throw in Indonesia and parts of the Philippines, plus, stir in the warlords, the drug traffickers, and the fanaticism of right-wing extremist religious leaders, whether Muslim, Jewish, or Christian.

Now tell me, where is the hope for world peace?

Many reputable globe-watchers see our world steadily polarizing into two major camps. Grossly oversimplified, the perceptions are: a radical Muslim world bent on religious dictatorship and global conquest, versus a "Judeo-Christian" world, defending pluralism and democracy, bent on Zionist and Christian fundamentalist interests. Of course, this is less and less an East-West polarization and more and more a radical fundamentalist polarization. Radical fringe Muslims and radical fringe Christians are now sprinkled throughout both hemispheres. But as the future grows progressively more ominous, again we ask: where is the hope?

Ah, do I hear a voice insisting, "It's Jesus! Jesus is the only hope of the world"? Oh, is he indeed? And where is the hard evidence of this? As my son puts it, "Dad, for two thousand years we have prayed, 'Thy will be done on earth even as it is in heaven.' But where is the evidence of this prayer being answered?"

LOCAL IRRELEVANCE

I felt despair challenging my faith on the home front, as well. A disturbing television documentary tested the notion that "the greater the Christian presence, the greater the benefit to the society at large." The host defined Dallas, Texas, as "the most Christian city in the world" (based on highest percentage of church attendance). But when he put Dallas under scrutiny on crime, justice, health care, infant mortality, educational quality, jobs, racial and economic equity, and the like, "Big D" rated toward the bottom of the heap. As one viewer observed, "By the time the host finished, no one would want to live in the 'most Christianized' city in America."

Then the other shoe fell. The host interviewed a number of Dallas's most respected Christian leaders and after walking them through his grim findings, he asked for their comments. Astoundingly, they all answered basically alike: "This is not really my concern; I am a *spiritual* leader, you know."

One person who watched the documentary observed, "My world began to crumble. . . . For years I have taught that it only takes twenty percent of a society to influence the other eighty percent to move in a given direction. But . . . Dallas has far more than twenty percent professing Christians. I reeled over the implications."[1]

Is this one clue to why the Christian faith is falling far behind population growth in North America? The United States is now the third most "unchurched" country on the planet![2]

RELIGION AS USUAL

Tell me again that Jesus is the only hope of the world.

Well, OK. I will. Let me take you by both hands, look you in the eye, and with a straight face say, "Oh, yes, if Jesus is not the hope of the world, then tell me, what is? The problem is not *Jesus*; it is *religion*!"

The impotence of the modern church in the face of personal, national, and global chaos is not, as G. K. Chesterton said, that "Christianity has been tried and found wanting, but that it has been found difficult and left untried."

For decades much of Christendom has not taken itself seriously as a viable *character changer*, much less as a *world-changing* force. Dallas Willard, in his now classic book *Spirit of the Disciplines*, says much of the Western church does not require following Christ in his example, spirit, and teachings as a condition of membership. "So far as the visible Christian institutions of our day are concerned, discipleship clearly is optional." Many churches have tended to settle for "membership without discipleship." Yet as we've seen before, the New Testament refers to Christ-followers as "Christian" only three times, but calls us "disciples" 269 times.

The hope of the world does not lie with "Christendom" but with Jesus Christ! And when the real Jesus stands up, hope also springs to its feet.

We must always keep our eyes focused on the guy asleep in the back of the boat. Look, he's sleeping. Yes, there's this violent storm upon us. Look at the winds and the waves! But just strap yourself to the mast, and keep your gaze on the man asleep up back in the boat.

RISING HOPE

Jesus has changed the world before, and will again. But he will work through shepherds from all backgrounds and traditions who:

- move away from micromanagement, permission withholding-granting, and status quo maintaining, and move toward "spiritual formation."

- acknowledge that "job one" is building persons rather than running organizations.

- use a leadership style moving toward shepherding, mentoring, and equipping.

- see that every Christian is a minister.

- equip persons for ministry, so that "each part works properly" and "the body builds itself up in love."

I also feel hope rising toward a generation of authentic spiritual leaders emerging across the community of faith who will not settle for "optional discipleship," nor fear the disciplines that open their lives to kingdom power.

I sense a rising army whose mission is to tap the life-changing power of heaven and passionately help others do the same—till hope spreads worldwide. Yes, an army!

Still, it may not take a whole army to change the world. One shepherd, strategically planted and God-anointed, can bring back hope to millions. *Even just one ordinary person like you or me!*

THE POWER OF ONE

In his book *The Body*, Charles Colson tells the gripping story of a little fellow named Telemachus. Telemachus lived in a monastery in Asia Minor toward the beginning of the fifth century. This little man, frail of body and simple of mind, had only one job: to tend the vegetable gardens and to pray, which he did faithfully for years . . . until he felt a strange compulsion.

Telemachus felt that God wanted him to go to Rome. He did not really know what Rome was, much less where it was or why he should go. But he could not shake the feeling. So finally, he tied his earthly possessions together in a little cloth, slung them over his shoulder, and set out for Rome. The trip took months. He traveled on foot and without a map.

Finally, Telemachus arrived in Rome in the spring of the year, just as the Romans were celebrating a military victory over the Goths. The government was passing out free food to the poor and free admission to the Coliseum, where the gladiators fought.

Telemachus found himself swept along with the crowd through the gates of the Coliseum and wound up seated in the nose-bleed section on the top row. Telemachus could scarcely believe the horror and bloodshed his eyes saw happening in the arena far below. Massive men saluted the Caesar as God and pledged to die in his honor. Then he saw these men hack each other to pieces with swords and run each other through with lances. He even saw naked men and women forced to fight to the death with wild beasts.

Telemachus stood and shouted at the top of his lungs, "In the name of Christ, desist!" But no one heard one little man's voice in the din of the crowd. So he elbowed his way down to the rail and shouted again, "In God's name, desist." The crowd laughed and shoved him over the rail, where he landed on the arena floor amid the thundering hooves and bloody, flailing swords.

By now the crowd had grown angry with this little interloper who dared to interrupt their games. So they stoned him. Telemachus fell on his face in the sand, and as a circle of crimson spread out from under him, a strange silence spread across the crowd. In the eerie quiet they watched as Telemachus raised himself one more time, and with what voice he had left repeated, "In the name of Christ, desist."

Somewhere the stands rustled as a mother took her children by the hands and headed for the exits. Then another. Then others, till finally hundreds streamed out the gates, leaving the Coliseum virtually empty. And that is the last time gladiatorial events were ever held in Rome.

Oh, yes! One disciple of authentic faith still can impact a world. How much more can one authentic, life-shaping, disciple-making shepherd change his part of the world!

Will you make yourself available to be that one? Will you have that kind of heart? A year from today, will you be distinguishably different from what you are right now? Will the world?

BLOWING THE DOORS OFF

Back to Larry King: When he asked Laura Bush how she could maintain faith in the fallout from 9/11, the First Lady replied, "In fact, our faith has only grown stronger." Her next words hit a sweet spot in my soul: "On our Christmas card this year, my husband and I printed words from the Twenty-seventh Psalm, 'I am still confident of this, I will see the goodness of the LORD in the land of the living.'"

Hope! Seeing the goodness of the Lord in the land of the living! Still confident!

Me too, Mrs. Bush. Me too!

Why? Because, above all, our optimism is rooted in our God—and our God is a God of surprises! In all of God's major movements, he has stunned the universe with surprise. No one could have anticipated what God would do next. Even the angels must have been caught off guard by the surprise of Creation. "Wow! Stars, planets, constellations, rattlesnakes, and roses—we never would have thought of any of that."

> In all of God's major movements, He has stunned the universe with surprise.

The Exodus, too, was a mega-surprise. God split the sea, led slaves out of bondage, and made them a nation. Who could have mapped this exit route or anticipated these mighty acts of God?

Surprise!

Again, in the first century AD, God showed up in a manger, ended up on a cross, rose up from a grave, fired up a Pentecost—and shattered global darkness with a million points of light. How utterly unpredictable from a human standpoint! The God of surprises stirred up the rushing of a mighty wind and blew history wide open . . .

and at the Reformation . . .

and on into our day of Restoration!

Surely, the God of surprises can and will awaken the church and shake the planet yet again. But he is depending on shepherds who see good things ahead.

The God of surprises is a God of hope. So for as long as you allow yourself to be called a shepherd, you *must* traffic in hope!

section seven: A HEART FLOODED WITH HOPE

We shepherds must respect and honor our past, our heritage, and those who have brought us this far. But we live in a new world now. We cannot go back. We must keep our eyes on the Chief Shepherd asleep in the back of the boat, dreaming of the ways God will work wonders tomorrow.

Man is a dreamer ever,

He glimpses the hills afar

And dreams of the things out yonder . . .

. . . when the God of surprises stirs up the winds of the Spirit and *blows our doors off!*

CARDIOVASCULAR WORKOUTS
FOR SHEPHERD HEARTS

1. List three reasons why we should allow ourselves to think that a God who demonstrated the power to change the world in the past cannot change our world now.

2. List three reasons to believe he can and will change our world again.

3. List the first three things you can do to be one of God's "world changers."

4. Write down the date and place you will do the first of these three things.

Be shepherds of God's flock that is under your care,
serving as overseers—not because you must,
but because you are willing, as God wants you to be;
not greedy for money, but eager to serve;
not lording it over those entrusted to you,
but being examples to the flock.
And when the Chief Shepherd appears,
you will receive the crown of glory
that will never fade away. . . .
Humble yourselves, therefore, under God's mighty hand,
that he may lift you up in due time.

—1 Peter 5:2–4, 6

epilogue

We have come to the end of this book. I have, of course, by no means spelled out everything to be desired in the heart of a shepherd. But I do hope that I have helped you to don a pair of "shepherd's heart" glasses so that for a lifetime you will gaze upon your world through those lenses. Searching for ways to deepen your own heart. Watching for Christian leaders with the heart of a shepherd. Longing to be a better shepherd.

Thomas Gray wrote, "Full many a flower is born to blush unseen, And waste its sweetness on the desert air."[1] Some souls who most exemplify the heart of a shepherd live and die virtually unnoticed by the public. So I leave you with just one real-life story of an unsung shepherd who has lovingly and faithfully shepherded God's flock in quiet places.

Somehow my mind keeps coming back to this letter from my dear friend Jack, himself a shepherd in Denver. It concerns his father, Mike.

Dad served as a shepherd in Laramie, Wyoming, for some thirty years. To work as a shepherd in a "mission church" environment can only be appreciated by those who have done so. I watched my dad struggle with limited personal resources, with the personalities of several different preachers who came and went over the years, and with serious personal health issues.

Dad suffered a major stroke in his early sixties and was disabled for the remaining few years of his life. Stress no doubt played a major role in his stroke. He so deeply felt the problems among the flock that he loved with all his heart.

When we sons saw this, we persuaded Dad and Mom to move from Laramie to Kerrville, Texas, hoping the calm of a retirement-community setting might bless them. They immediately became a vital part of a fine church there.

Shortly after, while he was visiting us in Colorado, Dad and I sat in the backyard one evening, enjoying a quiet visit. Dad said, "Son, the folks in Kerrville have asked me to serve as an elder. What do you think I should do?"

My thoughts raced to the protective issues. Hadn't God just recently answered our prayers to get Dad out of stress that had rendered him barely able to walk? It seemed crazy for him to get back into what we were so relieved to see him escape.

Knowing my dad, however, I suppressed my thoughts and simply responded, "Dad, there probably is no need to discuss this. We both know what you are going to do." I will forever remember his brief reply: "Well, Son, I just want to die with my boots on."

And he did!

To Mike and to the thousands of other faithful-but-unsung shepherds across the world: hats off to you. Thanks for being the kind of people that God-hungry people want to be like.

May your tribe increase.

notes

introduction: ASSUMPTIONS

1. Since we cannot honor all of those requests, we have developed a multimedia training package to go where we cannot. To order, visit www.lynnanderson.org.

one: THE HEART OF THE MATTER

1. "Character Matters," sermon given by Brad Tuggle at Oak Hills Church, San Antonio, Texas. February 19–20, 2005.

2. Hebrews 13:7.

3. 1 Samuel 16:7.

4. Psalm 78:70–72.

5. 1 Samuel 13:14, see Acts 13:22.

6. Psalm 27:8.

7. Psalm 19:14.

8. Psalm 51:10.

9. Isaiah 29:13, see Matthew 15:8.

10. Psalm 42:1–2.

11. Psalm 62:1–2.

12. Psalm 63:1.

13. Psalm 84:2.

14. Psalm 27:4.

15. Matthew 5:6.

16. As quoted by Robert Schnase, *Testing and Reclaiming Your Call to Ministry* (Nashville: Abingdon, 1991), 54.

17. Psalm 139:23–24.

18. As quoted by Frank Bateman Stanger, *Spiritual Formation in the Local Church* (Grand Rapids: Zondervan, 1989), 29.

two: A HEART COMPELLED BY THE GLORY OF GOD

1. Henri Nouwen, *The Way of the Heart: Desert Spirituality and Contemporary Ministry* (San Francisco: HarperSanFrancisco, Reprint edition, 1991).

2. See Ephesians 1:3–14.

3. Ephesians 3:21.

4. Exodus 33:12, 14.

5. Exodus 33:18.

6. See Exodus 33:12–23.

7. See Exodus 34:29–35.

8. Isaiah 6:1, 3, 5.

9. Ray Anderson, *Theological Foundations for Ministry* (Grand Rapids: T&T Clark, Ltd., 1979), 8.

10. Isaiah 6:11.

11. See Exodus 40:34–35.

12. See 1 Samuel 4:21–22.

13. Isaiah 42:1–3.

14. Isaiah 53:3.

15. Isaiah 53:5–6.

16. John 1:14.

17. Mark 10:45.

18. See Ephesians 1:22–23.

19. 2 Corinthians 3:18.

20. 1 John 4:12.

21. See Ephesians 3:16–19.

22. Ephesians 3:21.

23. Sandra D. Wilson, PhD, *Released from Shame: Recovery for Adult Children of Dysfunctional Families* (Downers Grove, Ill.: InterVarsity Press, 1990), 154.

three: A HEART ON ITS KNEES

1. "Leading from Our Knees," message by Rick Atchley, recorded at Church that Connects, Tulsa, OK, 2000.

2. 2 Peter 3:9.

3. Matthew 6:10.

4. Matthew 6:8.

5. Matthew 7:7.

6. Ibid.

7. Ephesians 3:20.

8. Romans 15:30.

9. Colossians 4:12.

10. Atchley, "Leading from Our Knees."

11. Ibid.

12. Ephesians 3:16.

13. Romans 8:11.

14. See Ephesians 3:16.

15. Psalm 127:1.

16. This American hymn is taken from a poem by Mrs. Love Maria Willis (1824-1908), published in *Tiffany's Monthly* (1856) with the title "Aspiration."

17. Gary Southern says, "I hand out *only* two books to shepherds or potential shepherds with whom I interact: 1.) Lynn Anderson's *They Smell Like Sheep* and 2.) *The Living Reminder* by Henri J. M. Nouwen. I view them as handbooks and 'how to' manuals on shepherding."

18. Henri Nouwen, *The Living Reminder* (San Francisco: Harper, 1984), 35–54.

19. Gary Southern is an elder in Denver, Colorado.

20. Atchley, "Leading from Our Knees."

four: A PRAYER PATH FOR SHEPHERDS

1. This chapter is a brief digest of my forthcoming book titled *Praying the Psalms*, to be released by New Leaf Publishers in 2007.

2. For a more extended discussion of this, see www.lynnanderson .org, archived under Hope from the Hills, "Learning to Pray."

five: A HEART IN SEARCH OF INTEGRITY

1. See John 20:31.

2. John 5:42.

3. John 5:44.

4. John Westerhoff, *Will Our Children Have Faith?* (New York: Seabury, 1976).

5. 2 Timothy 1:12.

6. Fyodor Dostoevsky, *The Brothers Karamazov* (New York: Farrar, Straus and Giroux, English translation: 1900).

7. Bulleted questions come from *The Leader's Journey* by Jim Herrington, R. Robert Creech, and Trisha Taylor (San Francisco: Jossey-Bass, 2003), 102.

six: PATHWAY OF INTEGRITY

1. Mark 15:34.

2. Stephen Crane, "The Wayfarer," *The Poems of Stephen Crane* (New York: Cooper Square Publishers, 1966), 94.

3. J. Oswald Sanders, *As a Word in Season*, trans. Ilse Lasche (Boston: Beacon Press, 1963).

4. John 5:44.

5. Psalm 78:71–72.

6. Psalm 51:6.

7. Psalm 32:2.

8. H. B. London Jr. and Neil B. Wiseman, *The Heart of a Great Pastor* (Ventura, Calif.: Regal Books, 1994), 151.

seven: A HEART SHAPED BY THE HOLINESS OF GOD

1. R. C. Sproul, *The Holiness of God* (Wheaton, Ill.: Tyndale, 1985), 55–57.

2. 1 Timothy 3:2.

3. Tuggle, "Character Matters."

4. 2 Corinthians 10:5.

5. Psalm 32:3–4.

6. Psalm 38:3, 7, 10.

7. Psalm 38:11.

8. 1 Peter 5:8–9.

9. Psalm 32:5.

10. As quoted by Derf Bergeman, "Sermon Preparation by Doing," *Circuit Rider*, September 1993, 17.

11. Psalm 32:6.

12. London and Wiseman, *Heart of a Great Pastor*, 228.

eight: A PATH TO PURITY

1. See 1 Timothy 1:15 KJV.

2. James 5:16.

3. Thomas B. White, *The Believer's Guide to Spiritual Warfare* (Ann Arbor, Mich.: Servant Publications, 1990), 118–19.

4. Matthew 28:20.

5. 1 Corinthians 10:13.

6. Matthew 7:11.

7. Psalm 19:12.

8. Psalm 30:11.

9. John Piper, *Future Grace* (Sisters, Ore.: Multnomah, 1995).

10. London and Wiseman, *Heart of a Great Pastor*, 228.

nine: IT'S ALL ABOUT PEOPLE

1. This chapter is adapted from *The Jesus Touch* by Lynn Anderson (West Monroe, La.: Howard Books, 2002). The book is essentially a training manual for teaching the people skills of Jesus.

2. Mark 12:30.

3. Mark 12:31.

4. 1 John 4:20.

5. Ezekiel 34:2–6.

6. Don and George shepherd together as elders in Dallas.

ten: A HEART FOR LOST AND HURTING PEOPLE

1. Eugene Peterson, *The Contemplative Pastor* (Carol Stream, Ill.: Word Publishing), 61–62.

2. Mark 2:17.

eleven: A HEART FOR THE WORD

1. See 2 Peter 1:12–15.

2. See 2 Peter 1:20–21.

3. John 5:39–40.

4. Acts 20:32.

5. James 1:21.

6. Psalm 119:106.

7. Romans 10:17.

8. Psalm 119:11.

9. Hebrews 4:12–13.

10. 1 Timothy 2:15.

11. 2 Timothy 3:16–17.

12. John 8:11.

13. 1 Corinthians 2:9 NASB.

14. Revelation 22:3–4.

twelve: A HEART FOR TEACHING THE WORD

1. Hebrews 13:7 MSG.

2. See Matthew 28:18–20.

3. Dallas Willard, *The Spirit of the Disciplines: Understanding How God changes Lives* (San Francisco: Harper & Row, 1988).

4. John Ortberg, "Holy Tension," *Leadership Magazine*, Winter 2004, 24–25.

5. "The Barna Group Discipleship Insights Revealed in New Book by George Barna," November 28, 2000, www.barna.org.

6. 1 Timothy 3:2.

7. See Matthew 28:18–20.

8. See 2 Timothy 2:2; Ephesians 4:11–13.

9. Ortberg, "Holy Tension," 24–25.

10. "Barna Group Discipleship."

11. Philippians 4:9.

12. 1 Corinthians 11:1.

13. Ortberg, "Holy Tension," 24–25.

14. 2 Timothy 2:2 NLT.

15. Ephesians 4:12 NKJV.

16. Ephesians 4:12 NIV.

17. Ephesians 4:11–12.

18. Gary is an elder in Denver.

fourteen: A HEART WITH HANDS

1. This figure, according to Carlin Romano, "Maybe not the best, but still first-rate," the *Philadelphia Enquirer*, December 26, 2004, www .philly.com/mld/inquirer/entertainment/books/10484323.htm.

2. Philippians 2:6–7.

3. See John 13:1–17.

4. John 13:3.

5. Richard Foster, *Celebration of Discipline* (New York: Harper & Row, 1978), 122.

6. Mark 1:40–42.

7. James 5:14.

fifteen: A BROKEN HEART

1. Ortberg, "Holy Tension," 24–25.

2. 1 Peter 5:4.

3. Isaiah 53:3.

4. John 15:20.

5. Mark 15:34.

6. Matthew 5:10–11.

7. James E. Dittes, *When the People Say No* (New York: Harper & Row, Publishers, 1979), 4–5.

8. Ibid, 2.

9. "That's My Soul Lying There," a poem by Earnest Stech, public domain.

10. 1 Corinthians 4:1–3.

11. Adapted from Joe Beam, *Seeing the Unseen* (West Monroe, La.: Howard Books, 1994).

12. Romans 5:5.

13. 2 Corinthians 1:3–5.

14. Landon Saunders, *The Wolf*, audiotape of lectures, March 1971. Online at http://www.wineskins.org/filter.asp?SID=2&fi_key=104&co_key=212.

sixteen: A HEART MOVING FROM WARRIOR TO LAMP

This chapter adapted from Anderson, *The Shepherd's Song*.

1. See 2 Samuel 21:15–17.

2. 1 Samuel 18:7.

3. Psalm 92:12, 14.

4. 2 Samuel 21:17.

5. 1 Timothy 4:12.

6. See 1 Timothy 4:6–8.

7. Psalm 37:25.

8. Job 12:12.

9. Russ Blowers, "Farewell to Arms," *Leaven Magazine*, Fall 2005.

seventeen: A HEART AT PEACE WITH AMBIGUITY

1. Charisa Hunter-Crump, "Prophetic Ministry," *Leaven Magazine*, Fall 2005.

2. Henry Van Dyke, *The Story of the Other Wise Man*, preface to the 1923 ed. (New York: Grossett & Dunlap, 1923), xv.

3. Proverbs 26:4–5.

4. Galatians 6:2, 5.

5. Galatians 5:1; Romans 6:18.

6. 1 Samuel 18:10; also see 16:14.

7. Isaiah 55:8.

8. 1 Kings 19:12 NKJV.

9. Psalm 46:10.

10. Psalm 1:4.

11. Samuel Miller, quoted by William C. Korley, "Finding Faith Again," *Mission Magazine*, November 1972, 6.

eighteen: A HEART THAT DOESN'T WRING ITS HANDS

1. John Eldredge, *Wild at Heart: Discovering the Secret of a Man's Soul* (Nashville: Nelson Books, 2001), 57.

2. See the excellent discussion by Gil Rendle, "The Illusion of Congregational 'Happiness,'" in *Conflict Management in Congregations* (Herndon, Va.: Alban Institute, 2001), 83–94.

3. 1 Timothy 3:2–3.

4. James 1:5–8.

5. See Matthew 8:23–27 KJV.

6. Edwin Friedman, *Generation to Generation: Family Process in Church and Synagogue* (New York: The Guilford Press, 1985).

7. See John 8:3–11.

8. Peter Steinke, *Healthy Congregations: A Systems Approach* (Alban Institute, 1996).

9. See Nehemiah 4:6–23.

10. Jim Herrington, R. Robert Creech, and Trisha Taylor, *The Leader's Journey* (San Francisco: Jossey-Bass, 2003), 17–18.

11. For help with this I recommend *The Leader's Journey*.

12. See Philippians 4:2–3.

13. Philippians 4:9.

14. Philippians 4:6–7.

15. Philippians 4:8.

16. The numbered list under "Additional Questions for Reflection" come from *The Leader's Journey*.

nineteen: A HEART OF ENCOURAGEMENT

1. Acts 4:36.

2. See Acts 4:36–37.

3. See Acts 9:26–30.

4. See Acts 11:19–24.

5. See Acts 11:25–30.

6. 2 Timothy 4:11.

7. Ellis Krogsgaard is an elder in Regina, Saskatchewan.

8. Randy Becton is an elder in Abilene, Texas.

twenty: A HEART THAT EXPECTS GOOD THINGS AHEAD

1. "Old Testament Template," by Landa Cope, www.ottemplate.org.

2. Dave Earley, "The Desperate Need for New Churches," https
:www.liberty.edu/media/1162/cmt, July 17, 2006.

epilogue

1. Thomas Gray, "Elegy Written in a Country Churchyard."

Transition your leadership team from managers to shepherds. Equip your leaders with shepherding skills.

If you...

- Desire more shepherding effectiveness
- Are a new elder and are feeling overwhelmed
- Want coaching in practical shepherding skills
- Wish to be a shepherd, not a manager, but don't know where to start
- Or are preparing new people to help you shepherd

...then the Spiritual Leadership Training Package is for you!

A twelve-week training package that is filled with hands-on shepherding and mentoring skills is now available! Applying the principles in *They Smell Like Sheep*, this training package incorporates video instruction and group interaction, but goes far beyond the book. Suitable for use in small or large groups, this spiritual leadership training is designed primarily for church leaders, but the basic biblical principles apply in all areas of spiritual leadership—parenting, friendship, small-group leadership, coaching—and even in the market place.

"Lynn Anderson's Spiritual Leadership Training Package is providing a common ground from which our six new leaders will shepherd our church family. The engaging format of the lessons has created unity and clarity. The sound biblical basis for the leadership principles presented in the series is comforting and convincing. This series is proving to be a wonderful blessing for our church family and our shepherding team."

—*Ross and Pamela Graham, Shepherding Team, Longview, Texas*

The multimedia interactive **training package** includes:

- Four VHS tapes *or* four DVDs
- A facilitator's guide
- A participant's workbook
- Access to the online Facilitator Forum

www.lynnanderson.org (210) 690-2597

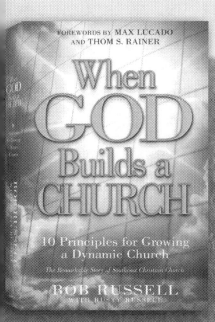
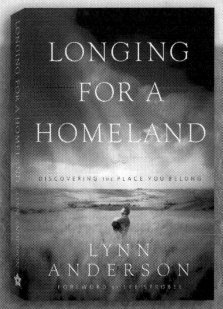